survive and thrive

winning against strategic threats to
your business

A Rotman Strategy Book

Edited by Joshua S. Gans and Sarah Kaplan

Toronto, Canada

Survive and Thrive: Winning Against Strategic Threats to Your Business

Published by Dog Ear Publishing
4011 Vincennes Rd
Indianapolis, IN 46268
www.dogearpublishing.net

ISBN: 978-1-4575-5665-4

Published by Rotman School Strategy Area (ON, Canada)

This book is printed on acid-free paper.

Printed in the United States of America

contents

acknowledgments

This book is an initiative of the Strategic Management Area at the Rotman School of Management, University of Toronto. We would like to thank the Rotman School (in particular, Vice Dean Ken Corts) for funding this initiative, as well as our Rotman colleagues for their support. We owe special thanks to Alden Hayashi for a wonderful editing job.

1.

introduction:
strategic threats
to survival

Joshua Gans and Sarah Kaplan

"And the winner is," said Warren Beatty as he handed the envelope to Faye Dunaway, "*La La Land!*" It was a moment that would define the Academy Awards ceremony in 2017 because the winner of the premier best picture award was not *La La Land* but the breakthrough movie *Moonlight*. Instead of celebrating the achievement of an African American-centered film about discrimination along multiple dimensions, the Oscars had become a farce. The scene was like a nightmare sequence, specifically for one firm: PricewaterhouseCoopers.

For decades, the accountants had been charged with keeping the list of Oscar winners safe and secret to be revealed at precisely the right moment. Every year, the two accountants given this important task were shown on television, purposely nerdy, purposely boring. Their job was to remain boring. The things that kept them up at night all involved getting too much attention.

Beatty had the wrong envelope (somehow for Best Actress rather than Best Picture). Thoughts of who was at fault immediately turned to PwC. The nightmare was real. The two accountants would never attend another ceremony. And PwC's careful branding was in tatters.

To be sure, nightmarish though this was, it was not of existential consequence. The accountants involved lost only their dignity but not their jobs. PwC would at worst lose the Academy as a customer. This was nothing compared to the destruction that had befallen Arthur Andersen more than a decade and a half earlier. Its errors led to the complete failure of the ninety-year-old company.

In 2001, Arthur Andersen was one of the big leading accounting firms. Those firms had an overwhelming share of the main corporate giants. In Andersen's case, that included one of the top ten most valued companies in the United States: Enron. Enron was an energy trading and finance company that had grown off the backs of energy deregulation in the 1980s and 1990s. It had a "go for broke" company attitude that made it the darling of many a popular management guru. But as it turned out, its financial foundations were weak. When these were exposed, Enron promptly failed. But as with the Academy Awards, attention turned quickly to the designated caretakers—in this case, the auditors: Arthur Andersen.

Overnight, other corporations lost confidence in the accounting company, employees in the thousands left to other accounting firms, and before any investigation was completed, Arthur Andersen was effectively no more; 85,000 employees and almost $10 billion in annual revenue went elsewhere. This was more than just a bankruptcy; there was simply nothing left.

It turned out that Andersen had left behind some years before the meticulous practices that had made it what it was. In other words, the failure was a symptom of a slow-moving and then long-standing problem. That problem, as it turned, out threatened their existence. So, unlike with PwC, the nightmare of Andersen was not one of embarrassment and the loss of a single client but went to the core of the firm itself.

This book is about these kinds of existential threats to businesses. It is about those potential crises that keep corporate leaders up at night. And, the problem with these threats is that they come from every direction.

Some actually come as a result of success. In the very week of PwC's Oscars debacle, Amazon faced a crisis of equal proportion and far great consequence. Aside from its highly successful online retail business, one of Amazon's most profitable divisions is the largest provider of cloud computing hosting services in the world. Amazon Web Services (AWS) powers not only myriad small start-ups but also many larger firms, from media outlets to Netflix to Google. It is everywhere.

On the morning of February 28, 2017, Amazon's Simple Storage Service (S3) team were engaged in routine debugging to fix a problem with their billing system. What was supposed to be a command to remove a small number of problematic servers had a typo in it that instead led to a large number of servers being removed, which then caused a cascade. Virtually the entire system went down. It was out for most of the day. With it, the Internet around the world shut down as businesses were unable to access stored data.

The system was eventually restored and Amazon promised to make changes so such an event would never occur again, but this reminded the world of its dependence on Amazon. While Amazon surely reaps some benefits—efficiency and competitiveness—from economies of scale, this incident may cause customers to diversify away from Amazon. In this case, Amazon did not face the loss of confidence that Arthur Andersen did, but the event did put Amazon on notice. What was supposed to be an unexciting, if lucrative, part of Amazon's business became far less so.

Technical issues will keep managers up at night, and as their businesses grow, managers will need to rise above the day-to-day crises and work out whether something more endemic is going on. That may be the case of AWS, but it was certainly the case for Uber, who, the very same week of the AWS crisis, revealed a problem of gender discrimination in its ranks.

The crisis—at least publicly—was triggered when an engineer, Susan Fowler, penned a blog post describing discrimination and harassment throughout the year she worked for Uber. This included a threat of dismissal when she reported these issues to Uber's human resource department. Such a dismissal would have been illegal. What the blog post revealed was not just a cultural problem within Uber but a formal structure that was aligned to perpetuate that cultural problem. This led to a new round of consumer boycotts to "#DeleteUber," as well as major legal issues and investigations.

Uber's strategic threats were baked into the organization. This was not a problem that could be fixed overnight, and it would require major changes. But for managers everywhere, the story should be a warning. If you have to wait until the crisis becomes public, it is too late; you have lost the ability to manage change on your own terms.

This book examines myriad strategic threats like those we have described above that could harm a business's existence:

- Despite detailed safety systems, BP's Deepwater Horizon well exploded, leading to the worst corporate environmental disaster in history and a $50 billion clean-up bill. (Chapter 2)
- Escalating healthcare expenses for current and former employees eventually contributed to bankrupt-

ing GM, as costs per car reached more than $1400. (Chapter 3)

- Walmart spent millions and suffered major reputational damage in the face of a 1.6-million-person class-action lawsuit filed for gender discrimination across the United States. (Chapter 4)
- A hotel's reputation was besmirched by potentially false TripAdvisor ratings, and bookings dropped precipitously. (Chapter 5)
- Disruptive innovations drove Blockbuster, Nokia, Kodak, and even the mighty Encyclopaedia Britannica out of business. (Chapter 6)
- The US nuclear industry faded to unimportance, with not a single plant breaking ground in the United States between 1977 and 2013, in part because of too-early lock-in on an inferior technology. (Chapter 7)
- A Toronto-founded startup, Atomwise, failed to get the funding and resources it needed because it did not locate in the right ecosystem and therefore had to move to Silicon Valley to succeed. (Chapter 8)
- Eli Lilly's performance declined sharply because of overinvestment in one growth model, even when that model had become counterproductive. (Chapter 9)
- A specialty foods venture—Evan Kristen Specialty Foods—lost financing because it focused exclusively

on the competitive dynamics in one segment of the value chain (consumer demand), at the expense of another (suppliers). (Chapter 10)

As the chapters in this book will demonstrate, the inability of companies to anticipate and respond adequately to these threats comes from some common organizational mistakes:

- **Mistake 1: Failing to appreciate interactions within systems.** Managers often appreciate only the superficial relationships between actors or events, without examining how interactions might compound problems in unexpected ways.
- **Mistake 2: Getting stuck in existing ways of doing business.** Companies become successful by honing their strategies and operations. In times of crisis, companies are often tempted to double down on these practices rather than seek out new responses, new growth models, or new methods.
- **Mistake 3: Falling victim to cognitive biases.** Despite the growing awareness that managers' judgment can be shaped by all sorts of biases, it is still exceedingly hard for managers to break themselves out of these traps. These biases can lead companies into crises and make it exceedingly hard for the companies to respond when crises hit.
- **Mistake 4: Getting derailed by short-term incentives.** The economic incentives to act—particularly

those driven by customer needs or demands—may blind organizations to risks that may arise.

The news we bring is that despite the acuity of these kinds of threats, companies can survive and thrive.

anticipate what you can; prepare for what you can't

The key is what we call structured anticipation: that is, understanding the risks and then building capabilities to ensure that when threats materialize, action is possible. Although crises may be far from pleasant, they do not have to create existential threats.

In the face of the organizational mistakes identified above, the chapters in this book suggest that two actions and two cautions form an approach to structured anticipation.

- **Action 1: Develop structured practices for anticipation.** Risk reviews, after-action reviews, anomaly-reporting systems, and the like can make the identification of potential risks more feasible. Without these structured practices in place, key information signals from the organization and the market will be lost.
- **Action 2. Create an organizational culture that encourages dissent.** Systems don't operate effectively without a supporting culture. A crucial way to anticipate risk is to look for anomalies and to

avoid discounting information and criticisms that don't fit with the organization's existing ways of doing business. Diversity of thought can be supported by diversity in teams and by safe spaces to bring up controversial ideas or information.

- **Caution 1: Beware of risk compensation.** Just as with increased safety features in cars, the temptation that comes with increased anticipatory practices is to take even more risks once the practices are in place. The goal of structured anticipation is not to encourage potentially foolish risks, but to anticipate internal and external threats while pursuing organizational performance.

- **Caution 2: Don't look for the easy way out.** Some companies want to buy their way out of problems. Others want to just do something that fits their existing way of doing business. More likely, the action necessary to fix the problem will obsolete or leapfrog today's practices and will require radical organizational change.

In each of the chapters in this book, you will find these themes recurring. For instance, while disasters such as oil spills and financial trading meltdowns can seem just like systems gone awry, Chapter 2 shows that organizations can prevent the occurrence of disasters by using systematic procedures to learn from smaller incidents and by creating cultures that allow anomalies and criticism to arise.

Where healthcare costs erode organizational productivity and corporate performance, Chapter 3 shows that these challenges can create innovation opportunities for those companies that can redefine health as prevention rather than medicalization.

With the increasing attention on the challenge of diversity and inclusiveness in organizations, companies can turn this challenge, as Chapter 4 argues, from a problem of compliance to an opportunity to win the war for talent.

In today's world, a poor review can spread quickly, bringing reputational damage just as quickly. Such damage can be perpetuated by managerial indecision about how to react when that damage occurs. Chapter 5 shows that by having a clear policy for managers to follow, companies can respond quickly and confidently implement corrections before things get out of control.

Although disruption has become a catchphrase as well as a "scary" concept for leaders of successful businesses, Chapter 6 shows that the classic disruptive innovations—those that appeal to a niche before invading your core space—can invariably be subject to a managed response. Firms with proactive capabilities can acquire firms that are competitive threats or can divert resources quickly to innovate on new paths.

For cases in which the development of complex, often breakthrough, technologies can be hampered by individual firms pursuing short-term incentives, Chapter 7 demonstrates how firms can coordinate to mitigate these incentive distortions and avoid lock-in on inferior solutions.

Where technology clusters provide crucial resources for innovation, Chapter 8 shows how firms both large and small can make the "do or die" decisions about where to locate their businesses in order to innovate, survive, and grow.

When companies must constantly reconfigure their resources to remain competitive, they can use systematic decision processes—as argued in Chapter 9—to select the best growth mode so they don't get stuck in old ways of doing business.

Finally, Chapter 10 shows that when it comes to competitive threats, with planning, competition can work for organizations as much as it might work against them. By realizing that your company is of value to other businesses in your value chain, you will be able to form coalitions with a broad group of partners to react when competitive threats arise.

***

This book is meant to be consumed all together or as individual chapters, according to the reader's interest. Across the chapters, you will find a wide variety of examples of strategic threats faced by companies. These crises often jeopardize the survival of the company, and the potential for these crises to emerge keeps leaders awake at night. Our goal with this collection of perspectives is to offer you, the organizational leader, some principles and practices for surviving and thriving in the face of strategic threats.

2.

managing the risk of catastrophic failure

Andrés Tilcsik

On April 20, 2010, mud began gushing out of the well onto the drilling floor at Deepwater Horizon. Seconds later, a geyser of water and mud sprayed up inside the derrick at the center of the giant rig; gas sensors went off everywhere, and the lights went out. One explosion was followed by a second, bigger blast, and a fireball hundreds of feet high enveloped the rig.[1] Eleven workers died in the accident that night, and the blowout that caused the explosions sent 200 million gallons of oil gushing into the Gulf of Mexico in one of the worst environmental disasters in history. BP's costs associated with the spill: more than $50 billion.[2]

Other catastrophes aren't physical but digital. When the markets opened on August 1, 2012, the Knight Capital Group was one of Wall Street's largest traders, but less than an hour later, the company was on the brink of collapse. A software glitch had caused the firm's trading system to go haywire and flood the market with four million unintended orders, resulting in Knight Capital acquiring several billion dollars in unwanted positions. When the firm eventually sold back those stocks, it had lost $460 million—roughly $200,000 *per each second* of the trading meltdown. By the next day, three-quarters of Knight Capital's market value had been erased. The firm scrambled to avoid collapse and was eventually acquired by a competitor.[3]

Disasters like BP's oil spill and Knight Capital's trading meltdown can threaten the very existence of even the largest corporations. And such failures aren't limited to high-stakes, exotic domains like deep-water drilling and electronic trading. From food-safety accidents in restaurant chains to defect recalls affecting car manufacturers, failures abound in ordinary industries and can devastate profits, trigger legal actions, and cause lasting reputational damage.[4]

To make matters worse, these dangers are increasing, according to many business leaders. In a recent survey of more than 1,000 executives in a wide range of industries, nearly 60 percent reported that the volume and complexity of the risks that their organizations face have increased substantially in the past half decade. At the same time, only a minority reported that their organizations had implemented complete firm-wide processes for enterprise risk management.[5] In this chapter, I describe some of the critical reasons that underlie the risks of catastrophic failure in organizations, then outline some solutions that research has suggested can help firms manage those risks.

unforgiving systems

In recent decades, many of the systems most critical to business activity—for example, supply chains, manufacturing and communications systems, power grids, and financial systems—have become substantially more complex in ways that have made them more vulnerable to major accidents. Three aspects of system complexity are particularly relevant for understanding catastrophic failures.

First, the elements of complex systems can interact in unintended and unanticipated ways, and as the number of components in a system increases, more opportunities for such unexpected effects arise. Take, for example, the interactions between newly deployed software and old dormant computer code (as in Knight Capital's meltdown), and between safety devices and various components of a physical system (as in the Deepwater Horizon accident).

Second, once a complex system begins to unravel, it's difficult to monitor and comprehend these unexpected interactions. In many cases, complex systems are opaque in the sense that their critical parts—a deep-water wellhead, the inner workings of an algorithmic trading system, or conditions in a firm's extended supply chain, for example—are hard to observe directly and in real time. In such cases, the health of the system might be measured only through indirect indicators that are not always perfectly accurate and may lag behind the current state.

Third, the elements of modern systems are often tightly coupled, meaning that failure of one function can quickly exert a significant effect on the rest of the system. Once a failure starts, it can spread rapidly across the whole system, leaving no time for operators, regulators, or managers to assess the situation, understand the nature of the issues, and mount an effective response. Unrestrained oil flows and unbridled trading systems, for example, can outpace anything but automated controls. And even when a problem spreads relatively slowly, complex feedback loops and the lack of direct indicators of system status can make it difficult for decision makers to comprehend and contain the unfolding problems.

These three aspects of complexity significantly increase the likelihood and potential impact of system failures. Unexpected interactions make it difficult for executives to anticipate what will cause things to go wrong. The inability to observe those interactions makes it hard to understand what is happening within a system. And tight coupling between the different parts of a system means that, even if executives understand what's happening, they face the challenge of having to pause the system in time to prevent a cascade of increasingly serious failures.

This doesn't mean, of course, that catastrophic failures must occur regularly. In fact, in a particular system, risk-management policies and safety devices tend to ensure that major accidents occur only rarely. But occasionally, unanticipated interactions between different parts of a complex system can overwhelm operators and defeat critical safety systems, leading to a disaster.

When a system is prone to complex interactions, its exact condition isn't directly observable, its various components are tightly coupled, it tends to be unforgiving, and the penalties for human errors and organizational weaknesses can be huge. In other words, any mistakes that an organization operating in a simpler environment might be able to absorb with impunity can turn into big problems when a complex system is involved.[6]

cognitive challenges

Cognitive biases—fundamental hardwired limitations in how the human mind processes information—can lead to mistakes, oversights, and misunderstandings in nearly everything we do, yet most of the time, their effects are limited. In relatively simple systems—like an assembly line that we can directly observe, control, and, if necessary, shut down—these biases tend to be less dangerous than in complex systems. If things go wrong because of human error, we can quickly spot problems and intervene. In many modern systems, however, the problems these biases cause are hard to detect and comprehend in real time, and their ripples can travel fast and far. Moreover, these persistent and widespread biases often rear their ugly heads precisely when we need to make quick intuitive decisions during crises or when we must reason about the low-probability events that underlie many accidents.

The *availability heuristic*, for example, leads us to overestimate the probability of events that we can easily recall. As a consequence, we tend to focus on events with which we have personal experience, those that are described in particularly vivid terms, or those that have occurred recently. Conversely, we tend to underestimate the probability of events that have yet to happen or that are outside our typical frame of reference. In other words, we tend to prepare for the last disaster rather than the next one. This is particularly troubling because of the emergent nature of risky systems; often, the failures that occur are novel, making it difficult for us to consider the full range of vulnerabilities.[7]

The availability heuristic is exacerbated by *confirmation bias*, which leads us to selectively seek information that supports our existing beliefs and to discard contradictory evidence. Thus, executives who believe that a process is robust and well-functioning may continue to believe so, even as near misses mount or as employees raise concerns to the contrary. And when those same executives stress-test their systems or decisions and receive ambiguous results, they are inclined to ignore any information that clashes with their prior beliefs.[8]

Likewise, as a result of *change blindness*, we sometimes fail to detect crucial changes even if they are right in front of our eyes. That is, if we aren't specifically looking for them, we can easily miss large, unexpected changes in our environment.[9] Recognizing small, nuanced changes—such as the subtle initial signs of an emerging crisis—is even harder.

A related problem is systematic *overconfidence* on the part of decision makers, which tends to increase with subject-matter expertise. Decades of research has found that experts—from financial analysts to CIA analysts—often overestimate the accuracy and precision of their forecasts. And such overconfidence seems to be most pronounced when reasoning about rare events in uncertain environments.[10]

Lastly, once a crisis is unfolding, *plan continuation bias* causes us to continue with our original or habitual plans of action even when conditions change and those plans become problematic. This bias tends to be particularly strong when only a few remaining steps are required to complete our original plan, and it can prevent us from noticing subtle cues indicating that our plan is no longer viable.[11]

organizational challenges

Organizational processes are another major source of errors that can throw sand in the gears of modern systems and, under the wrong conditions, become the basis of major failures. An important problem in this regard is the phenomenon known as *risk creep*. This is the process through which an unacceptably risky practice gradually becomes acceptable. A behavior that deviates from organizational policies—for example, failing to follow some of the more arduous steps of a complicated protocol or giving approval to a decision that *almost* meets safety standards—rarely results in disaster the first time it occurs. Indeed, such deviations can often be repeated time and time again without catastrophic results, but as the deviance continues without consequences, it can develop into an accepted norm. What used to be seen as errors, lapses, and mistakes become informal codes of conduct, and it becomes a routine part of the job to pursue an unacceptably high-risk trading strategy or to be alone in a control center despite a formal two-person rule. Sometimes, not even harrowing near misses—cases in which dumb luck intervenes to avert disaster—halt this process. In fact, executives and managers often see averted failure not as a warning but as evidence of resilience. After all, the system seems to have worked: Disaster was prevented. But in complex systems, risk creep leads to errors and undue risk taking that can one day trigger a chain of other breakdowns.[12]

A related phenomenon is what accident researchers call *risk compensation* and what economists call *moral hazard.* When organizations establish procedures to enhance safety and system stability, their employees may take more risks because they know that a safety mechanism is in place. In one study, for example, taxi drivers were randomly assigned cabs with or without anti-lock brakes, and those driving cars equipped with them tended to drive faster, accelerate more rapidly, and make sharper turns than their peers driving otherwise comparable vehicles. It seems that the drivers compensated for the existence of safety systems by taking more risks.[13] A similar phenomenon might have occurred aboard Deepwater Horizon, where the presence of a blowout preventer—a critical piece of safety equipment—may have contributed to excessive risk taking.[14]

Another source of potentially fatal errors—call it the *normality presumption*—stems from the way organizations plan for and respond to unexpected events. Although business-continuity planning has been a hot topic in recent years, research on the contingency plans that organizations actually do develop provides little cause for optimism. Accident researchers have shown that plans are often predicated on an implicit assumption that, save for the focal event itself, an organization will be in its usual high-functioning state: An oil spill, a security breach, or a computer-system meltdown, for instance, will occur on an otherwise calm day when all the resources necessary for a response will be available within the normally expected time frame.[15] In reality, however, crises tend to strike when organizations are *not* operating as effectively as they would on a normal day, and anxious and sleep-deprived managers, constantly ringing phones, and the lingering shock of a sudden unexpected event is hardly an ideal combination for cool-headed decisions and error-free communication.

Many contingency plans also suffer from *illusory redundancy*: a situation in which a backup plan or system is vulnerable to the same disruptions as the main system it's meant to protect.[16] A company that has multiple suppliers of critical components, for example, may suffer shortages if those suppliers are located nearby and are all vulnerable to the same natural disaster or political instability. Similarly, a firm that loses service from a telecommunications provider will achieve little actual redundancy if its backup carrier depends on some of the same faulty facilities that the primary provider uses.

solutions

So, what can executives do to reduce the risk of catastrophic failures in their organizations? Traditional risk-management steps—such as instituting rules and controls, planning scenarios, and bringing in additional experts—can be quite helpful, but they have their limitations as the complexity increases. For example, a rule-based approach—identifying the things that could go wrong, instituting procedures to prevent them, and enforcing those procedures through monitoring—often fails to capture the breadth of potential risks and may instead foster a punitive culture that causes people to conceal risks. The use of scenario planning to identify risks is a more sophisticated approach, but it has problems of its own, sometimes leading decision makers to focus on a potentially narrow set of risks and responses based on scenarios that are vivid and easy to imagine. All too often, scenario planning also fails to capture the messy complexity of interconnected systems and organizations, as well as the chaos and fallibility of crisis responses. Research in numerous industries likewise reveals fundamental limits of relying on expert ability. For example, teams dominated by subject-matter experts are often vulnerable to group overconfidence and might suppress valuable input from non-expert skeptics. Such group dynamics are especially likely to yield bad outcomes in complex and uncertain environments.

At the same time, researchers are increasingly uncovering other interventions that can improve decisions, strengthen complex systems, and reduce catastrophic risks.[17] The following list summarizes some of those best practices.

1. **Learn from incidents.** In complex systems, it's impossible to predict all of the possible paths to catastrophe. Even so, there are often emerging signals that can bring to light any interactions and risks that might otherwise be unexpected and hidden. Indeed, a timeline of the

weeks and months leading up to a major failure is often a history of smaller failures, near misses, glaring irregularities, and other indications that something might be amiss. Incident tracking is a powerful way to learn from such signals, and there are notable success cases.[18] In healthcare and aviation, for example, effective incident-reporting systems help managers sort through the overwhelming haystack of possible warning signs to identify sources of potentially catastrophic errors. In recent years, such systems have proliferated in other industries as well. But these systems are effective only if employees feel safe enough to report issues and if the output is actually used to generate insights and to effect change. To make this possible, it's essential to designate a specific group with sufficient understanding of operational concerns to sort through, analyze, and prioritize incoming information. In the absence of this, insights can be lost even when critical data are available. Moreover, once information is recorded and analyzed, people must use it to generate insights about the root causes of those incidents and to fix problems without delay, rather than simply relegating the information to a risk report. Emerging insights can then be disseminated throughout the organization. When used in this way, incident-reporting systems can enable decision makers to *anomalize*—that is, to treat minor errors and lapses as distinctive and potentially significant details rather than as normal, familiar events.[19]

2.   Encourage dissent. Insiders often have serious reservations about the decisions or procedures in place well before a major accident, but they either fail to share these concerns or are ignored by managers. Many of those who observe these indications—typically, employees on the front lines—feel uncomfortable disclosing errors, expressing dissenting views, and questioning established procedures. To counter these tendencies, it's important for leaders to cultivate *psychological safety:* a shared belief among team members that the group will not admonish or penalize individuals for speaking up and challenging established procedures or widely held views. Psychological safety requires a climate in which team members trust and respect one another regardless of differences in their formal status. Research has shown that through their words and actions, executives can do a great deal to foster psychological safety in a team or even within an entire organization.[20] This requires that leaders credibly signal that they are willing to consider and address challenging questions and dissenting voices openly and productively, rather than defensively. These kinds of leadership behaviors help demonstrate that it's safe to raise questions, to admit mistakes, and to disagree with the team's consensus—critical steps in understanding where hidden dangers might be lurking in a complex system.

3.   Use structured decision tools. One way to reduce the number of small errors that might cascade into larger failures is to mitigate the effect of cognitive biases in decision making. The use of structured decision tools, rather than intuitive thinking, can lessen the influence of some of those biases. Cognitive psychologists, for example, have proposed a list of twelve questions that executives can use to detect and minimize the effect of cognitive biases when making major decisions based on a recommendation from their team. For example, is the worst case bad enough? Were dissenting opinions adequately explored? And could the diagnosis of the situation have been overly influenced by salient analogies? Many of these questions are quite straightforward and seemingly obvious, but in practice, they are rarely raised explicitly. A checklist ensures that these questions are actually considered, thus helping executives apply quality control to their decisions.[21] Similarly, decision tools can reduce the effect of cognitive biases in predictions. For instance, a simple tool called Subjective Probability Interval EStimates (SPIES) has been shown to produce fewer overconfident estimates than do unstructured, intuitive forecasting approaches.[22]

4.   Diversify teams. Teams composed of individuals with diverse professional backgrounds and expertise can be an effective risk-management strategy. Research on bank boards, for example, suggests that banks with some non-expert directors—those with backgrounds in other fields, such as in law, the public sector, or the military—tend to be less likely to fail than banks with directors who all come from a banking background. It seems that having a mix of industry experts and non-experts can serve as an effective safeguard against overconfidence on a board. These outsiders often raise inconvenient questions and force bankers on the board to justify their proposals and explain why formerly unacceptable risks might have become acceptable.[23] In addition, even surface-level diversity—diversity in team members' visible characteristics, such as sex, age, and race—might help reduce the overconfidence of decision makers. Recent research, for example, suggests that the mere presence of ethnic diversity can reduce overconfidence in the actions of others, thus fostering greater scrutiny and more deliberate thinking.[24]

5. Conduct risk reviews. A risk review is a structured audit of an organization by external investigators who gather qualitative and quantitative data to uncover hidden and unexpected risks to the organization. The investigators, who are typically independent experts on risk management in complex systems and organizations, begin the review by conducting confidential interviews with a variety of personnel at different levels in the organizational hierarchy, from higher-level executives to junior employees working on the front lines. The goal of these interviews is to reveal potential risks that might not be visible at a given hierarchical level or within a particular organizational silo. The interviews can also provide an indication of the willingness of employees to share their concerns and dissenting opinions with supervisors. Next, to examine the most important issues raised in the confidential interview process, the investigators gather additional qualitative or quantitative data from surveys, further interviews, or the organization's archives. Because a risk review leverages independent generalist experts and cuts across hierarchical and bureaucratic boundaries within the organization, it's particularly suitable for uncovering risks that are created by internal decision-making processes and organizational structures. It's also an effective guard against risk creep. Although the gradual slide toward increasingly risky practices tends to be imperceptible to insiders, outsiders can often recognize it and help ensure that unacceptable risks are challenged and mitigated.[25] Of course, a risk review will be effective only if executives are open to the investigators' conclusions, even if that information might occasionally be uncomfortable, disconcerting, and perhaps painful to hear. Otherwise, the investigators' main advantage—their independent external perspective, allowing them to question industry and company assumptions and conventional practices, to poke holes in arguments, and to disagree with the existing consensus—can easily be lost.[26]

6.   **Develop more realistic contingency plans.** It's essential for organizations to develop robust crisis planning and response capabilities. During the process, executives need to recognize that estimates for worst-case scenarios are often explicitly or implicitly built from information

that is biased by observations of recent orderly behavior and by the assumption that the mitigations outlined in a crisis-response plan will actually work. To identify possible planning failures, decision makers can rely on independent outsiders to stress-test critical estimates in plans, explore extreme scenarios, and challenge optimistic assumptions about organizational performance during a crisis. This can lead to more realistic worst-case scenarios and the development of more-robust crisis-response plans. To avoid the pitfall of illusory redundancy, managers should carefully assess whether their backup plans are susceptible to the same risks as their regular operations. Rather than quickly narrowing their focus to the technical merits and challenges of a particular solution, executives should define the broad goals of the intended redundancy and identify counterexamples for which backup measures might also be vulnerable. The goal is for people to shift their perspectives and see redundancy as a vulnerable part of the system rather than as an invincible panacea.

These recommendations are not rocket science. They also don't require large financial investments or expensive technologies. That, however, does not mean that they are easy to implement. Indeed, getting organizations to heed dissenting voices, learn from small anomalies, and open themselves to independent scrutiny can be a difficult leadership challenge. And it's often extremely hard to change deeply ingrained routines for planning and decision making.

The good news is that these interventions don't necessarily clash with other key organizational priorities. Although it may seem that paying more attention to risk reduction, accident prevention, and safety will necessarily undermine a firm's focus on innovation and profits, the above-described solutions can actually enhance multiple organizational objectives. Team psychological safety, for example, is not only an effective safeguard against catastrophic risks but also a critical factor in the effectiveness and creativity of teams, as recent research at Google has revealed.[27] Similarly, interventions that minimize the effect of cognitive biases in decision making not only can reduce catastrophic risks but also might increase investment returns.[28] Better management of catastrophic risks, it seems, can also lead to better management more generally.

endnotes

1. "Escape from the Deepwater Horizon," *New York Times*, available at http://www.nytimes.com/video (last accessed June 20, 2016).
2. "BP to Pay $18.7 Billion for Deepwater Horizon Oil Spill," *New York Times*, available at www.nytimes.com (last accessed June 20, 2016).
3. C. Clearfield, A. Tilcsik, and B. Berman, "Preventing Crashes: Lessons for the SEC from the Airline Industry," *Harvard Kennedy School Review* (2015), available at www.harvardkennedyschoolreview.com (last accessed June 20, 2016); and "SEC Charges Knight Capital with Violations of Market Access Rule," Securities and Exchange Commission (2013), available at https://www.sec.gov/News/PressRelease/Detail/PressRelease/137053 9879795 (last accessed June 20, 2016).

4. See, for example, S. Strom, "Chipotle Food-Safety Issues Drag Down Profits," *New York Times* (2014), available at www.nytimes.com (last accessed June 20, 2016); and B. Vlasic, "Hurt by Vehicle Recalls, G.M.'s Profit Falls 85%," *New York Times* (2014), available at www.nytimes.com (last accessed June 20, 2016).

5. M. Beasley, B. Branson, and B. Hancock, "2015 Report on the Current State of Enterprise Risk Management: Update on Trends and Opportunities," North Carolina State Enterprise Risk Management Initiative, available at https://erm.ncsu.edu/library/article/current-state-erm-2015.

6. This section draws heavily on ideas from C. Perrow, *Normal Accidents: Living with High Risk Technologies*, revised edition (Princeton, NJ: Princeton University Press, 1999); and C. Clearfield and J. Weatherall, "Why the Flash Crash Really Matters," *Nautilus* (2015), available at http://nautil.us/issue/23/dominoes/why-the-flash-crash-really-matters (last accessed June 20, 2016).

7. A. Tversky and D. Kahneman, "Availability: A Heuristic for Judging Frequency and Probability," *Cognitive Psychology* 5, no. 2 (1973): 207–232.

8. R.S. Nickerson, "Confirmation Bias: A Ubiquitous Phenomenon in Many Guises," *Review of General Psychology* 2, no. 2 (1998): 175–220.

9. D. J. Simons and D. T. Levin, "Change Blindness," *Trends in Cognitive Sciences* 1, no. 7 (1997): 261–267.

10. See E. Angner, "Economists as Experts: Overconfidence in Theory and Practice," *Journal of Economic Methodology* 13, no. 1 (2006): 1–24; S.W. Lin and V.M. Bier, "A Study of Expert Overconfidence," *Reliability Engineering & System Safety* 93, no. 5 (2008): 711–721; and A. I. Shlyakhter, D.M. Kammen, C.L. Broido, and R. Wilson, "Quantifying the Credibility of Energy Projections from Trends in Past Data—The United States Energy Sector," *Energy Policy* 22, no. 2 (1994): 119–130.

11. K. Dismukes, B.A. Berman, and L.D. Loukopoulos, *The Limits of Expertise: Rethinking Pilot Error and the Causes of Airline Accidents* (Surrey, UK: Ashgate Publishing, 2007).

12. D. Vaughan, *The Challenger Launch Decision: Risky Technology, Culture, and Deviance at NASA* (Chicago: University of Chicago Press, 1997).

13. M. Aschenbrenner and B. Biehl, "Improved Safety Through Improved Technical Measures? Empirical Studies Regarding Risk Compensation Processes in Relation to Anti-lock Braking Systems," in R.M. Trimpop and G.J.S. Wilde, editors, *Challenges to Accident Prevention: The Issue of Risk Compensation Behavior* (Groningen, the Netherlands: Styx Publications, 1994).

14. See M.A. Roberto, "Blowout Preventers, BP, and Compensatory Behavior," available at http://michael-roberto.blogspot.hu/2010/07/blowout-preventers-bp-and-compensatory.html (last accessed June 20, 2016).

15. L. Clarke, *Mission Improbable: Using Fantasy Documents to Tame Disaster* (Chicago: University of Chicago Press, 1999).

16. C. Clearfield, "Managing the Criticality of Catastrophic Events" (2013), *Forbes*, available at http://www.forbes.com/sites/chrisclearfield/2013/10/11/managing-the-criticality-of-catastrophic-events/#1bf7b7d12236 (last accessed June 20, 2016).

17. For a more exhaustive treatment of useful interventions and their implementation, see C. Clearfield and A. Tilcsik, *Meltdown* (New York: Penguin Press, forthcoming).

18. C.H. Tinsley, R.L. Dillon, and P.M. Madsen, "How to Avoid Catastrophe," *Harvard Business Review* 89, no. 4 (2011): 90–97.

19. K.M. Sutcliffe and M.K. Christianson, "Managing for the Unexpected," University of Michigan, Ross School of Business, Executive White Paper Series (2013), available at http://positiveorgs.bus.umich.edu/wp-content/uploads/managing_unexpected_sutcliffe.pdf (last accessed June 20, 2016).

20. A. Edmondson, "Psychological Safety and Learning Behavior in Work Teams," *Administrative Science Quarterly* 44, no. 2 (1999): 350–383; and M.A. Roberto, "Lessons from Everest: The Interaction of Cognitive Bias, Psychological Safety, and System Complexity," *California Management Review* 45, no. 1 (2002): 136–158.

21. D. Kahneman, D. Lovallo, and O. Sibony, "Before You Make that Big Decision," *Harvard Business Review* 89, no. 6 (2011): 50–60.

22. U. Haran, D.A. Moore, and C.K. Morewedge, "A Simple Remedy for Overprecision in Judgment," *Judgment and Decision Making* 5, no. 7 (2010): 467.

23. J. Almandoz and A. Tilcsik. 2016. "When Experts Become Liabilities: Domain Experts on Boards and Organizational Failure." *Academy of Management Journal*, 59: 1124-1149.

24. S.S. Levine, E.P. Apfelbaum, M. Bernard, V.L. Bartelt, E.J. Zajac, and D. Stark, "Ethnic Diversity Deflates Price Bubbles," *Proceedings of the National Academy of Sciences* 111, no. 52 (2014): 18524–18529.

25. See D. Vaughan, *The Challenger Launch Decision: Risky Technology, Culture, and Deviance at NASA* (Chicago: University of Chicago Press, 1997).

26. See C. Perrow, "Organizing to Reduce the Vulnerabilities of Complexity," *Journal of Contingencies and Crisis Management* 7, no. 3 (1999): 150–155.

27. C. Duhigg, "What Google Learned from Its Quest to Build the Perfect Team," *New York Times Magazine* (2016), available at http://www.nytimes.com (last accessed on June 20, 2016).
28. D. Lovallo and O. Sibony, "The Case for Behavioral Strategy," *McKinsey Quarterly* (March 2010): 30–43.

surviving the threat of healthcare

Anita M. McGahan

In October 2005, General Motors and the United Auto Workers reached a compromise to reduce GM cash outlays on healthcare benefits for active and retired personnel by an estimated $1 billion. The agreement was hailed as a victory for both parties because it would lower the company's costs while preserving jobs. But the seeds of GM's demise had already been sown. Even in that very same year, the company's annual report had warned investors that escalating healthcare costs were an existential threat:

> Health care in the United States is one of our biggest competitive challenges, and if we do not make progress on structurally fixing this issue, it could be a long-term threat to our company. In

2005, GM was challenged with the compound impact of escalating health-care cost rates and falling discount rates used to determine future health-care liabilities. As a result of these factors, in 2005, GM's U.S. other postretirement employee benefits (OPEB) expense, consisting of retiree health care and life insurance, increased to $5.3 billion, an increase of more than $1 billion from 2004.

Four years later, on June 1, 2009, General Motors filed for bankruptcy in the United States, Canada, and Ontario. In hindsight, it is clear that the structural issue of escalating healthcare costs had indeed set the foundation for failure. As the *Economist* explained, "Every year the cost of retired workers' health care diverted billions of dollars from developing new models and added $1,400 to the cost of each car compared with those made in Asian and European transplants."[1] That's $1,400 per car. In other words, the company's past success created obligations that eventually took the company down.

GM's problems are not unique. Over the years, escalating healthcare costs have been cited in the bankruptcies of Kodak, Xerox, and Data General, among others. Of course, healthcare expenditures and issues have many implications for firms. Healthcare benefits can help attract and retain talent, drive productivity, and reinforce a company's values and image of being social responsible. As the cost of providing healthcare escalates, however, the achievement of competitive advantage through each of these mechanisms becomes more difficult. The escalating costs of healthcare also shape the context in which businesses operate, such as when UK voters opted for the Brexit based in part on the argument that leaving the European Union would free resources to open one acute-care hospital per week in the country. Who can forget those photos of London busses with signs proclaiming in huge letters, "We send the EU £350 million a week; let's fund our NHS [National Health System] instead"?

In many markets, escalating healthcare costs also create opportunities for companies. Innovation is rewarded in the pharmaceutical, medical-device manufacturing, healthcare provision, acute-care, insurance, tertiary healthcare, food-manufacturing, restaurant, information-technology, and lifestyle-support industries. On cost-benefit arguments, companies in each of these sectors disrupt incumbents by introducing innovative products and services that improve health, reduce the likelihood of illness, and/or reduce the cost of care. Consider the following examples. Pharmaceutical companies argue that the prophylactic administration of cholesterol-lowering medicine averts heart attacks and thus is justified both as a lower-cost and more humane intervention than post-attack acute care. Medical-device manufacturers have been introducing cheaper and more accurate dental-imaging machines than those currently in use developed decades ago. Food manufacturers tout organic and low-fat options. Information-technology companies have analyzed health data to provide more accurate and comprehensive assessments than were previously available. And lifestyle-support companies now offer holistic "wellness" solutions designed to reduce the costs of healthcare by averting illness through better fitness, healthier diets, mental-health support, and other means.

Thus, just as escalating healthcare costs have threatened companies like General Motors, they have also created a powerful incentive for firms to innovate in various markets. So, what will dominate? Will the opportunities outpace the threats? Can companies innovate to improve quality of life and to lower healthcare costs quickly enough to counteract the threats to general business from escalating healthcare costs? And more to the point, what will it take to prevent additional bankruptcies?

description of the threat

A fundamental point—one that is central to the sustainability of our way of life—is that the cost of healthcare must go down in real terms. We simply cannot afford the healthcare system that we have now. The good news is that lowering the cost of healthcare is possible, even with the technologies that are prevalent today.

A few statistics are in order. The cost of healthcare now is barely affordable. In 2015, the estimated expenditure on healthcare per person in the United States was approaching $10,000 per person—about 17 percent of the

GDP. The equivalent figures for Canada and the UK were about half that level—nevertheless, a high percentage of income.

Many older, established companies in the healthcare industry have developed strategies that essentially emphasize the exporting of Western healthcare systems into emerging markets, but this approach will eventually hit a wall. The hard truth is that healthcare even in wealthy countries is rapidly becoming unaffordable, and the same type of system will undoubtedly be unaffordable in less-wealthy countries.

To be sure, many of the innovations pioneered by established companies have had a significant impact in reducing costs. Kaiser Permanente, for example, has been a pioneer in innovative healthcare administration. Additionally, the industry has certainly seen its fair share of breakthrough medicines, devices, protocols, and holistic approaches. The problem, though, is that these innovations have not been large or fast enough to alleviate the problem fully. The hard truth is that, despite the successes that have accumulated to date, the healthcare system in place in most wealthy countries has become costlier each year. Put simply: Innovations have made a difference, but the ship continues to sink. If everyone in the world were to have the same healthcare as available today in Switzerland, the entirety of world GDP would be exhausted by the bill.

The heart of the problem is that our current model of healthcare was conceived and built in the late nineteenth and early twentieth centuries on principles that reflected industrialization: The human person was conceived as an essentially healthy being, with the challenges of disease and illness remediated by medical care. This medicalization of healthcare meant that interventions generally occurred after patients became symptomatic. In other words, we went to doctors after we got sick, not before. The incentives associated with the system were therefore developed to reward the remediation of illness: Doctors got paid the most when they saw sick patients, not well ones. Moreover, the private ownership of pharmacological information under the patent system created a powerful incentive for private companies to invest in the costly development of annuity medicines—that is, therapies that could be administered to chronically ill patients over long periods of time. For their part, medical-device companies were incentivized to develop equipment that their customers—such as the owners of acute-care facilities—could justify by a return on investment in new therapies. Even the term "medical school" pointed to the roles of physicians as medicators rather than as health providers.

In his brilliant book *Being Mortal*, Atul Gawande describes the consequences of the systemic problem in human terms:

You don't have to spend much time with the elderly or those with terminal illness to see how often medicine fails the people it is supposed to help. The

waning days of our lives are given over to treatments that addle our brains and sap our bodies for
a sliver's chance of benefit. They are spent in institutions—nursing homes and intensive-care units—
where regimented, anonymous routines cut us off
from all the things that matter to us in life. Our re-
luctance to honestly examine the experience of
aging and dying has increased the harm we inflict
on people and denied them the basic comforts they
most need. Lacking a coherent view of how people
might live successfully all the way to their very end,
we have allowed our fates to be controlled by the
imperatives of medicine, technology, and strangers.[2]

Gawande teaches us that our system has evolved to
solve one problem after another by mostly well-intentioned
actors working from the resources available at the time the
problem was confronted. We have created a healthcare system that reflects our values, which are of economy, ration-
ality, technology, and a kind of self-determinism that leads
to isolation of the elderly.

What is needed to counteract the threat of escalating
costs is a new way of thinking about healthcare that rests
on a twenty-first-century mindset about what is possible
in both human and economic terms. My students know
what to do in order to avoid a heart attack at age fifty and
to avert other types of cardiovascular conditions and can-
cer: eat right, go to the gym, sleep enough, stop smoking,

drink in moderation, develop strong relationships, and reduce stress. When I ask them why they don't do these things, they tell me variations of the following: "It's too hard"; "On a Friday night, my friends expect me to go drinking with them"; "I can't find the energy to go to the gym"; and "I'm so worried about finding a job that I stay up all night studying." These students are on a track to suffer the same kinds of diseases and at the same stages of life as my generation.

To support the practices that my students know are best for them, we need an entirely different way of approaching healthcare. Incentives must change so patients tell physicians about risky behavior and physicians are rewarded for helping them stay healthy. Products and services that sustain health must be as abundantly available as those that damage health, which means that these sustaining products and services must be profitable and desirable. As just one example, vaccines must become profitable enough to compete with annuity drugs in order to attract the best scientific talent to work on them. Physician culture must change to emphasize health and quality of life. Patients must be better educated about the potential adverse consequences of various courses of care. Medical schools must become health schools, and they must offer courses of education that yield qualified physician assistants, nurses, and community workers as health providers. The dissemination of knowledge about heath must have safeguards to prevent any undermining by private conflicts of interest. National conversations must develop on late-life quality of life. In short, the whole system needs to be redesigned to emphasize prevention, the early diagnosis of illness, comprehensive treatment, social support, mental health, social relationships, and meaningful work. Lastly, the new system must be designed to capitalize on digital and other technologies to reduce radically the cost of healthcare, and it must be both better and cheaper.

As difficult as each of these individual changes is by itself, the transition from the established system to a new system is the greatest challenge. Already, a thousand great ideas for transforming the system are out there, but implementation has been stymied by the pervasiveness of entrenched mindsets, vested interests, and the old ways of doing things. Today, when innovations designed to improve quality of life and lower costs are introduced into healthcare systems, they are typically crushed by an established administrative structure. Even simple, commonsense interventions have been difficult to implement. In short, shifting to a new system gradually is nearly impossible, and yet no responsible society would allow the disbanding of established healthcare systems to enable an entirely new approach. So, then, how do we move forward quickly without losing what we have? And how do we make progress in less-wealthy countries that seek access to the essential medicines but clearly cannot afford the systemic apparatus that took down GM? Or, in the terms used by my colleague Joshua Gans, professor at the Rotman School of

Management: How can we avoid disruption while encouraging the system change required to make progress?

managerial strategies to counter the threat

Answering these difficult questions will require decades of work in every affected sector, yet even now, rigorous managerial research suggests several fruitful ways to begin, and already a number of principles have emerged:

1. The goal for change must be maintaining and sustaining human health. Healthcare organizations—like organizations in all other industries—tend toward processes that sustain the organization. This occurs for a range of reasons: preservation of jobs, belief in purpose, commitment to value creation for patients, preservation of legacy, fear of change, and concerns about risk. Especially in healthcare, successful organizations may put themselves out of business over time as their missions become fulfilled. Consider the following example: President Jimmy Carter has had a passionate commitment to the eradication of guinea-worm disease, and the Carter Center's anti-leishmaniasis program has been organized to pursue that goal. President Carter would like nothing more than to put this program out of business by achieving that mission, so the goal here is to sustain health rather than sustain the organization itself. That type of perspective needs to be purposefully cultivated on a larger scale. That is, people should always be mindful that, in many cases, their ultimate success can be achieved only when their organization—or, more frequently, a program of certain activities—is no longer needed.

2. Climate change threatens human health and, as a consequence, the entire healthcare system that we have in place today. The effects are already in motion: droughts that diminish agricultural productivity, storms and warm temperatures that together promote infection, weather disasters that create humanitarian emergencies, and pollution that harms crucial ecosystems. As climate change progresses, the demands on the health sector are escalating. In response, the following are crucial priorities: improving systems for producing and distributing high-quality food, identifying weather events in advance of their occurrence, and configuring effective humanitarian responses on an international basis.

3. The future of healthcare is digital. The list of opportunities for improving health systems through digitization is so extensive that any attempt to capture that scope is daunting. Indeed, digital tools can be deployed in myriad applications for identifying health issues, preventing the transmission of infectious diseases, improving the quality of life of the elderly, and administering effective health treatments. Despite the range of opportunity, the health system often resists digitization in complex ways. For example, in one hospital in downtown Toronto, new applications cannot be adopted because the enterprise computing system is too old to accommodate them. In other cases, legitimate concerns about privacy and effective diagnoses must be addressed before progress can occur. And in still other situations, digitization requires the development of new protocols that physicians resist because they are concerned about the risks for patients and the administrative burden of too much change. Our research suggests that relatively few providers actively resist digitization out of self-interest or laziness or ignorance or stubbornness. Rather, the problem of implementation is often one of organizational siloes and the absence of relevant digital and medical expertise in the right places at the right times. A major opportunity exists in addressing these issues.

4. Achieving coordinated change in healthcare will require public leadership. The fundamental reason for this is that human health problems—injuries, communicable diseases, and non-communicable diseases—are so prevalent than they cannot be covered by any single organization in any place in the world. Delivering healthcare is essentially a local endeavor, but human health problems are global in nature and character. Thus, improving the quality and reducing the cost of the healthcare system requires the global dissemination of best practices that can emerge anywhere. Public leadership is essential for identifying these practices and for compelling the adoption of those practices internationally.

5. Iconic pioneers can inspire a generation. Pioneers such as global-health physician Dr. Paul Farmer, the emergency-medical organization *Médicins Sans Frontières*, and various scientists have been motivating the next generation of health professionals. My students—Millennials, mostly—are readily inspired by breakthrough leaders who cultivate health even at the expense of their own career progress and financial advancement. Small experiments that succeed, including Farmer's successes in Cange, Haiti, demonstrate to the world, and particularly to inspired young leaders, that systemic progress is possible. As evidence of success accumulates, concerns about the risk of change in large organizations will tend to diminish.

6. Popularizing small, well-designed experiments is critical to progress. Randomized controlled trials are the currency of innovation in healthcare. This method for legitimizing change is designed to ensure not only that the proposed changes work but also that they are the best available among all those that might be effective. Management changes become compelling to health providers and health scientists when those changes are supported by the results of randomized controlled trials. To meet the evidentiary burden, successful small-scale experiments must accumulate to the point that costly randomized controlled trials become worthwhile.

7. **The private sector plays a crucial role in scaling.**
The private sector, by pursuing profitable interventions,
supports the scaling of effective and efficient new approaches through decentralized coordination. In healthcare, the mechanisms that support private activity include
intellectual property protections (namely, patents) and
rules of law that limit liability and enable insurance. These
institutions have led to a concentration of innovation
around medicines and medical devices. New types of institutions are likely needed to support innovation in pri-
vate-sector health delivery. Identifying and developing
them is central to achieving scale in innovation in this sector.

8. **Sustainability in health systems depends on a new
national and international conversation about the goal
of healthcare**. What are we trying to achieve? Atul
Gawande has described how most of us living in wealthy
countries will die in institutions in ways that are relatively
isolated and medicalized.[3] Is this what constitutes the quality of life that we want healthcare to deliver? What are the
alternatives? How do we make better decisions during
health crises? And how do we set up systems to support the
quality of life that we want? Answering these questions is
critical to understanding what sustainability means.

conclusion

How can a company avoid the fate of GM? Even though discussion about the future of healthcare is in its infancy, some answers are already evident. Specifically, providing employees with access to healthcare that emphasizes prevention, quality of life, and intensive and early treatment is both cost-effective and humane. And competing effectively for talent will depend on supporting innovative and enlightened approaches to health both in the workplace and through insurance programs.

That said, GM's greatest untapped opportunity in this domain may not have been in economizing or innovating in healthcare provisions for its workers and pensioners. Like those of companies in many other sectors, GM's products and services influence human health both directly and indirectly. What would have happened to GM if it had offered vehicles that dramatically reduced carbon emissions or resisted injury using self-driving technologies? Of course, GM did pursue some of these opportunities, yet the company likely could have done more. Could the automaker, for instance, have led a national and international conversation on innovative road design, car-sharing programs, and car-recycling opportunities? Each of these initiatives, pursued strategically and thoughtfully, might have made GM a leader in healthy transportation systems.

The simple truth is that *all* companies can benefit by designing products and services aligned with the principles of health transformation described in this chapter. Choices about workplace policies are just the tip of the iceberg. In every sector of the economy, products and the offering of services designed to support human health are simply more sustainable than those that are not, and in general, those companies that understand this basic concept will be better positioned to prosper over the long term than those firms that do not.

endnotes

1. "The bankruptcy of General Motors: A giant falls," *The Economist* (June 4, 2009)
2. Atul Gawande, *Being Mortal: Illness, Medicine. and What Matters in the End* (Profile Books, 2014).
3. Atul Gawande, *Being Mortal: Illness, Medicine. and What Matters in the End* (Profile Books, 2014).

the challenge of gender diversity

Sarah Kaplan

In June 2001, Betty Dukes, a Walmart worker in California, filed a class-action lawsuit claiming sex discrimination on behalf of 1.6 million women currently or previously employed at Walmart. The potential liability for the giant retailer was considerable: more than $1 billion.[1] Over the next decade, the company found itself fighting all the way through to the US Supreme Court, which eventually ruled in 2011 in the retailer's favor. Still, Walmart suffered substantial hits to its bottom line as well as to its reputation. The estimated total legal costs of the lawsuit and related gender-discrimination settlements—which continue to this day in various class actions at the state level—exceed several hundred million dollars. The cost to the company's brand is hard to calculate, but by the mid-2000s, when media and activist attention were at their height, Walmart's public favorability rating was falling; the number-one reason was "bad labor practices, not good to employees."[2]

Walmart was hardly alone in its struggles with gender equality. In the fall of 2014, Microsoft CEO Satya Nadella was at a conference celebrating women in computing when he advised women to "trust in karma" when hoping for a raise. This set off an Internet firestorm in which both he and Microsoft were criticized for their poor record on attracting, retaining, and promoting women. Indeed, just a week earlier, Microsoft had published data indicating that its global female workforce stood at only 29 percent overall, with much of that in the retail segment, only 17 percent in technology jobs, and just 17 percent in leadership roles. The backlash in social media prompted swift apologies from Nadella, both to the public and to his more than 100,000 employees. Less than a year later, though, Microsoft was hit with its own class-action lawsuit brought by Katie Moussouris on behalf of female technical employees who claimed that the company's systems for evaluation led to discriminatory outcomes. Recent similar lawsuits have buffeted the world of technology, from Ellen Pao's well-publicized suit against Kleiner Perkins Caufield & Byers, to legal actions taken against Facebook and Twitter.

Whether in retail, high tech, or another industry, companies are vulnerable to attack if their actions, intended or not, lead to discriminatory processes and outcomes. These attacks can be quite detrimental to an organization's objectives, from the direct legal costs, to the impact on brand and reputation, to the inability to attract and retain the best talent. And on the flip side, there's mounting evidence that gender diversity is associated with positive outcomes such as increased innovation, risk mitigation, and improved financial performance.

Most companies are aware of these issues and recognize that even beyond the business case, gender diversity is an important objective in its own right, yet even in 2017, organizations have struggled to make progress. In fact, many efforts have not only failed to improve gender diversity but have sometimes backfired, leading to stagnation or negative outcomes. In this chapter, I outline the underlying reasons that discriminatory outcomes occur even with the best of intentions. I then examine the paradoxes associated with many efforts to effect change, and I outline some of the more promising solutions suggested by the research.

a stubborn problem

If so many companies are well-intentioned in their efforts, why has the gender gap been so difficult to close? There are three reasons.

First, it's important to recognize that gender is a primary frame through which we all see the world. Whether or not we personally endorse particular stereotypes about male and female behavior or characteristics, these frames will still influence our actions. According to sociologists, this is because we need these common cultural beliefs in order to coordinate our actions. For psychologists, these are unconscious biases built into our thinking from the time we enter the social world.[3] For most of us (men and women alike), our attitudes and responses are shaped instantaneously by these frames. In other words, we are on autopilot.

Second, gender shapes how we value and evaluate women's contributions, and in many contexts, gender has become a status marker devaluing that which is female. Research has shown time and again that simply adding in a marker for the female gender can lead to lower valuations and evaluations, whether in placing investments or in hiring and promotion decisions. Specifically, equal business plans get half the money if the pitch is narrated by a woman. Equivalent résumés get fewer callbacks if the name at the top is female. Indeed, in many male-dominated contexts such as business and finance, feminization can actually be used as a weapon against men who transgress or upset the social order.[4]

Third, gendered frames are embedded in a socially complex system, such that these biases are built into all of the ways we do business. What appears to be neutral can in fact be gendered. We think, for example, that the pitch process for picking investments in new ventures is meritocratic, with the best ideas receiving the most funding. But if pitching is seen as a typically male activity, then men are likely to be seen as inherently more successful at doing it. And, women, even (or especially) if they "pitch like a man," may still be seen as less competent. Or consider the recent class-action lawsuit against Microsoft, which focuses on the "stacking" process for ranking employees. Unfortunately, such forced ranking procedures may conflate self-confidence with competence and, because men are socialized to act more self-confidently (whether they actually are more self-confident is a different matter), they are likely to get ranked higher in the stack.

For the above three reasons, companies have found it difficult to make progress in gender equality. In the 1970s and 1980s, both North America and Europe saw considerable advances in achieving workplace equality for women, but progress has since stagnated. The lowest-hanging fruits—such as ensuring that women could have their own checking accounts or eliminating the distinction between "jobs for women" and "jobs for men" in the help-wanted ads—have already been harvested. What's left is the tough work of rooting out the effects of gendered frames in the systems in which we operate.

slow progress

A major reason progress has been slow is the unintended consequences of the recommendations that people have made and the policies that organizations have implemented. Let's start with "leaning in." Sheryl Sandberg's bestselling book *Lean In* has helped focus the conversation around gender in the workplace. Its primary advice is for women to lean in: ask for raises, put themselves up for promotions, seek out job opportunities, and so on. These recommendations emerge from research showing that "women don't ask."[5] Said differently, women are socialized not to ask. Although the message to lean in has resonated with many women who have felt disempowered in the workplace, the challenge with this recommendation is that it focuses on asking women to *buck* the system rather than targeting how companies could *change* the system. This can be problematic because the system is designed to push back. Remember that gender is a primary frame and that we are socialized to see women as pushy or strident when they make requests that would seem reasonable coming from men. Research has shown that when women do not conform to gender expectations, they pay a penalty. They are accused of having "sharp elbows" or are subject to sexual harassment. Perhaps this is why Satya Nadella, the Microsoft CEO, recommended that women place their trust in karma for raises. He must have at least suspected how fraught "leaning in" can be.[6]

An obvious recommendation, then, is for companies to help people become aware of their unconscious biases to safeguard against them. This solution has become very popular in top corporations, with massive investments in unconscious bias training. More than 17 million people have taken Harvard's Implicit Association Test, and the results show that three-fourths of us have at least some unconscious association of men with careers and women with family life. It would seem like a positive step to help people become aware of these frames through which they see the world.

What could be wrong with such an initiative? Research has shown that, unaccompanied by other, more substantive, measures, diversity training (including unconscious bias testing) is mainly ineffective. Some studies have even found a negative backlash because people often have adverse reactions to this type of training. Even trickier, diversity training has become a catchall for every kind of difference in an organization, from background to race and ethnicity, to gender, to education, and to functional experience. Again, on its face, that might not seem problematic, but research suggests that focusing on such a broad set of diversity characteristics means that diversity training may actually draw attention *away* from gender.[7]

Firms can also try to shape individual action through compelling statements about the importance of diversity to their organizations. These statements are meant to signal both internally and externally that diversity is a priority in the organization's efforts to attract, retain, and promote people. The hope is that these statements will create a set of norms that will shape the actions of employees.

Research suggests, however, that what companies say and what they do are often decoupled. One reason is that the mere presence of a diversity statement may lead people in positions of privilege to lower their guard against bias. That is, when people believe they are working in a meritocratic environment, they will be less likely to consider whether they, themselves, might be making biased decisions. Further, under these conditions, those in privilege (whites and men) tend to have harsher reactions to claims of discrimination. The claims may even feel outrageous to those who believe they are operating in a gender- or race-blind meritocracy.

On the other side, people who might benefit from policies promoting diversity can take diversity statements as a signal that they do not need to have their guard up either. For example, although many people of color "whiten" their résumés when applying for jobs, they tend to do it less when the employer has a powerful diversity statement. If firms do not practice what they preach, these applicants will, ironically, experience more discrimination from a firm with a diversity statement than from a firm without one. Applicants don't whiten their résumés so biased employers are therefore more likely to discriminate against them.[8]

So, if solutions focusing on individuals are not particularly effective, what about solutions that address the system directly? There are two classes of interventions: those that use affirmative action to give greater consideration to disadvantaged groups, and those that focus on making management systems and structures more truly "objective" to curb the effects of biases without giving any social groups what can be perceived as special advantages. Each has its limitations.

Affirmative-action programs have been a primary and often useful structural solution to bias. The goal of such initiatives (also known as employment-equity programs) is to create a level playing field for women and other protected classes through procedures designed to eliminate unlawful discrimination. But here too, the implementation of such approaches has been troubled when not framed correctly. Affirmative-action approaches may be useful in uncovering implicit biases in evaluation criteria and in encouraging more creative approaches to attracting and retaining talent, but research has shown that those in positions of privilege (men when it comes to gender, and whites when it comes to race) tend to dislike these programs because they interpret the programs as threats. This has led, in the United States especially, to many high-profile legal challenges to good-faith efforts to achieve diversity.

On the other side of the equation, women who benefit (or are seen to benefit) from such programs can suffer from workplace stigma. The logic goes something like this: The women must not be as good as their male counterparts, because they got their jobs only because they are female—especially if these women were recruited based on quota and not on merit.[9] These effects are based on perceptions, but, evidence suggests, not on reality. For example, a study of political quota systems in Sweden shows that quotas actually increased the average quality of everyone—men and women—in the talent pool (in part by weeding out mediocre men who had previously benefited from the bias against women in the system).[10]

Other solutions that have sought to limit managerial discretion in hiring and promotion—the use of job tests for selecting employees, strict interview guidelines for questioning job candidates, performance evaluations for identifying employees to promote, and grievance procedures for stopping discriminatory managers—can also be subject to backlash. These kinds of more "data driven" and procedural approaches are seen to be important solutions to discriminatory outcomes. Indeed, grievance systems are recommended as a remediation in more than one-third of discrimination lawsuit settlements, yet when organizational policies and procedures are seen as infringing on job autonomy, managers are more likely to resist their implementation and will even sabotage the results.[11]

what to do

So, what does this mean for Walmart or Microsoft or any company that would like to make progress on gender equality? It seems that every well-meaning intervention, on either the individual or organizational level, is fraught with pitfalls.

Let's start with a caveat: There are no silver bullets. When sociologist Bill Bielby served as an expert witness on the side of the claimants in the Dukes v. Walmart case and the American Sociological Association subsequently filed an *amicus* brief with the US Supreme Court in support of the use of sociological research as valid evidence, a controversial debate ensued: Did scholars really know what policies and practices would reduce bias? The answer, as can be seen from the evidence on pitfalls above, is a partial "no."[12] That is, there's no "one size fits all" solution, because organizational context and culture matter. Further, each country or locality may have different legal constraints on action. What is possible in Canada regarding affirmative action (employment equity) may no longer be possible in the United States because of a series of recent court cases constraining these types of policies.

Moreover, even if some policies do seem, on average, to have positive effects, we also have to recognize that those same policies can have unintended consequences *unless* they are actively monitored and managed. It's not that women should refrain from leaning in; it's also that management should recognize that the system needs to be changed so that leaning in doesn't lead to retribution. It's not that firms should eschew diversity training; it's also that without complementary organizational changes, such training could be detrimental. And it's not that firms should avoid proclaiming that diversity is valued in their organizations; it's also that these statements should be matched with real actions.

Those caveats notwithstanding, recent research suggests that the following actions can have positive effects on increasing gender equity in organizations.[13]

1. **Ensure networking, mentorship, and sponsorship.** Networks are an important source of social capital. People get jobs and promotions in part because of their formal and informal connections. Mentorships can also help build social capital by giving women or other minorities access to guidance that they may not have otherwise received because of their weaker networks. Even more powerfully, sponsorships can get women and minorities considered for jobs, projects, and promotions. Many firms have developed "employee resource groups" around gender, ethnicity, and other categories. These are aimed at creating the powerful networks, mentorships, and sponsorships that are valuable in career development. The latest research suggests that these groups are not the solution to inequity but that they do have modestly positive effects on reducing discrimination and creating opportunity.[14]

2. **Engage managers in promoting diversity.** Although managers tend to resist constraints on their autonomy, they are much more likely to be supportive of special recruitment and training programs. Often known as "soft" affirmative action, efforts to encourage women to apply to certain programs or to receive training in specific skills

tend to be viewed more favorably by those in privileged positions. In addition, research suggests that engaging men in such efforts will make them more likely to support diversity. One reason is cognitive dissonance: When someone becomes involved in these programs, it becomes difficult for that individual to simultaneously believe that the programs are not useful. Another reason is knowledge: Being involved in programs helps men understand the dynamics at play that lead to women being at a disadvantage. These initiatives work particularly well if they are positioned not as giving women (or minorities) special advantages but rather as correctives to privileges that men (or whites) have.

3. Increase transparency for job seekers and managers. Transparency has two positive effects. First, it provides those seeking jobs or promotions with more information about opportunities. In the Walmart class-action suit, one of the claims focused on the lack of transparency in job postings such that women reportedly didn't even know to apply and therefore would not be considered for promotions. When job postings are made available to all, it becomes less likely that the privileged networks of those in leadership will be the only sources of potential workers to fill positions. Second, transparency makes managers accountable for their actions. When people know they are being measured or monitored for their choices, they tend to work actively to control their own biases, whether conscious or unconscious. Transparency also opens up the possibility for discussion around why progress is or is not being made.

4. Monitor results. Research has shown that most reforms work better with monitoring, which can come in many forms. Within firms, the creation of a high-level role of diversity manager can increase compliance and improve progress because there's now a person with clear authority to track results. Studies have also shown that companies subject to regulations because they are government contractors also do better because the government monitors their diversity performance. Similarly, pressure from the public can lead to greater compliance. The recent push for technology firms such as Google, Facebook, and Microsoft to publish their statistics on gender, race, and employment incentivizes them to do better. Once it is known that only 17 percent of women are in leadership roles (as at Microsoft), the company will feel pressure to report better results in subsequent years. In each case, monitoring acts as a catalyst. Studies have shown that even when certain policies might limit managerial discretion and thus be subject to resistance by managers, these policies might still have a positive outcome *if* they are accompanied by some form of monitoring.[15]

Thus far, this chapter on gender equality hasn't mentioned maternity and paternity leave. Recently, there's been a great deal of attention focused on improving access to paid maternity leave in places like the United States (the only developed country to not have guaranteed paid leave of any kind) and on increasing the availability and use of paternity leave. Recognizing the biological reality that women are the ones who bear children and are most physically involved in childcare in the earliest days (through breastfeeding), it's clear that work policies need to accommodate this reality, through both adequate maternity leave and access to appropriate facilities for pumping milk when back at work. The challenge, of course, is that such accommodations become highly gendered and therefore associated with lower status. This means that because of the status implications, men are less likely to take advantage of any policies that would allow them to take a leave. A solution proposed by many is to ensure that men also have real access to paternity or family-leave accommodations and perhaps make it a requirement (as has been done in Sweden, where the mother cannot take the extra days reserved for the father) so that the status implications are lessened.

There's no doubt that family-leave policies and other efforts to take into account people's responsibilities outside their jobs are crucial foundations for achieving gender equity at work. Sweden ranks at the top of gender equity in the world, so these policies, though not silver bullets, do help. We know, however, that this is not the full solution. Even in Sweden, the gender pay gap of 14 percent is close to the Organisation for Economic Co-operation and Development (OECD) average of 15 percent, and it's even larger among parents (21 percent). Further, in Sweden, only 10 percent of CEO positions of the top 1,000 companies are held by women and only 24 percent of board members are women.[16] This demonstrates the perniciousness of gender as a primary frame: Even in contexts that for years have had family-friendly policies in place for women *and* men, discriminatory outcomes persist.

This is where the four recommendations come into play. Without active policies for promoting sponsorship, engaging managers in diversity objectives, increasing transparency, and monitoring results, we are unlikely to achieve much change. Knowledge of the pitfalls should not be used as an excuse for inaction. Instead, awareness of the potential unintended consequences can help any organization innovate in developing an approach that is tailored to its own culture and context, resulting in true progress toward greater gender equality.

endnotes

1. 1. A. Zimmerman and N. Koppel, "Bias Suit Advances Against Wal-Mart," *Wall Street Journal* (April 27, 2010), available at http://www.wsj.com/articles/SB100014240527487034652045752080035548858 (last accessed April 26, 2016).
2. "Results of Wal-Mart Watch/Westhill 2007 Public Opinion Survey," Wal-Mart Watch, available at http://walmartwatch.com/wp-content/blogs.dir/2/files/pdf/polling_summary.pdf (last accessed April 26, 2016).

3. See M.R. Banaji and A.G. Greenwald, *Blindspot: Hidden Biases of Good People* (New York: Delacorte Press, 2013); and C.L. Ridgeway, "Framed Before We Know It: How Gender Shapes Social Relations," *Gender & Society* 23, no. 2 (2009): 145–160.
4. See A.W. Brooks, L. Huang, S.W. Kearney, and F.E. Murray, "Investors Prefer Entrepreneurial Ventures Pitched by Attractive Men," *Proceedings of the National Academy of Sciences of the United States of America* 111, no. 12 (2014): 4427–4431; R.E. Steinpreis, K.A. Anders, and D. Ritzke, "The Impact of Gender on the Review of the Curricula Vitae of Job Applicants and Tenure Candidates: A National Empirical Study," *Sex Roles* 41, nos. 7–8 (1999): 509–528; and C.H. Enloe, *Seriously!: Investigating Crashes and Crises as if Women Mattered* (Berkeley, CA: University of California Press, 2013).
5. See S. Sandberg, *Lean In: Women, Work, and the Will to Lead* (New York: Alfred A. Knopf, 2013); and L. Babcock and S. Laschever, *Women Don't Ask: Negotiation and the Gender Divide* (Princeton, NJ: Princeton University Press, 2003).
6. See A.H. Eagly and S.J. Karau, "Role Congruity Theory of Prejudice Toward Female Leaders," *Psychological Review* 109, no. 3 (2002): 573–598; M.E. Heilman, A.S. Wallen, D. Fuchs, and M.M. Tamkins, "Penalties for Success: Reactions to Women Who Succeed at Male Gender-Typed Tasks," *Journal of Applied Psychology* 89, no. 3 (2004): 416–427; and J.L. Berdahl, "The Sexual Harassment of Uppity Women," *Journal of Applied Psychology* 92, no. 2 (2007): 425–437.
7. A. Kalev, F. Dobbin, and E. Kelly, "Best Practices or Best Guesses? Assessing the Efficacy of Corporate Affirmative Action and Diversity Policies," *American Sociological Review* 71, no. 4 (2006): 589–617.
8. D. Pager and L. Quillian, "Walking the Talk? What Employers Say Versus What They Do," *American Sociological Review* 70, no. 3 (2005): 355–380; C.R. Kaiser, B. Major, I. Jurcevic, T.L. Dover, L.M. Brady, and J.R. Shapiro, "Presumed Fair: Ironic Effects of Organizational Diversity Structures," *Journal of Personality and Social Psychology* 104, no. 3 (2013): 504–519; and S.K. Kang, K.A. DeCelles, A. Tilcsik, and S. Jun, "Whitened Résumés: Race and Self-Presentation in the Labor Market," *Administrative Science Quarterly* (forthcoming).
9. See M.E. Heilman, "Sex Stereotypes and Their Effects in the Workplace: What We Know and What We Don't Know," *Journal of Social Behavior and Personality* 10, no. 6 (1995): 3–26; M.E. Heilman, J.A. Lucas, and C.J. Block, "Presumed Incompetent—Stigmatization and Affirmative-Action Efforts," *Journal of Applied Psychology*

77, no. 4 (1992): 536–544; and M.M. Unzueta, A.S. Gutierrez, and N. Ghavami, "How Believing in Affirmative Action Quotas Affects White Women's Self-Image," *Journal of Experimental Social Psychology* 46, no. 1 (2010): 120–126.

10. See T. Besley, O. Folke, T. Persson, and J. Rickne, "Gender Quotas and the Crisis of the Mediocre Man: Theory and Evidence from Sweden," *American Economic Review* (forthcoming).

11. See F. Dobbin, D. Schrage, and A. Kalev, "Rage Against the Iron Cage: The Varied Effects of Bureaucratic Personnel Reforms on Diversity," *American Sociological Review* 80, no. 5 (2015): 1014–1044.

12. See J.B. Sorensen and A.J. Sharkey, "The Perils of False Certainty: A Comment on the ASA Amicus Brief in Dukes vs. Wal-Mart," *Sociological Methods & Research* 40, no. 4 (2011): 635–645.

13. Much of this list is drawn from F. Dobbin, D. Schrage, and A. Kalev, "Rage Against the Iron Cage: The Varied Effects of Bureaucratic Personnel Reforms on Diversity," *American Sociological Review* 80, no. 5 (2015): 1014–1044.

14. F. Briscoe and S. Safford, "The Nixon-in-China Effect: Activism, Imitation, and the Institutionalization of Contentious Practices." *Administrative Science Quarterly* 53, no. 3 (2008): 460–491; and A. Kalev, F. Dobbin, and E. Kelly. "Best Practices or Best Guesses? Assessing the Efficacy of Corporate Affirmative Action and Diversity Policies," *American Sociological Review* 71, no. 4 (2006): 589–617.

15. F. Dobbin, D. Schrage, and A. Kalev, "Rage Against the Iron Cage: The Varied Effects of Bureaucratic Personnel Reforms on Diversity," *American Sociological Review* 80, no. 5 (2015): 1014–1044.

16. "Gender Equality in Sweden," website of the Swedish government, available at https://sweden.se/society/gender-equality-in-sweden/ (last accessed April 26, 2016).

5

reputation in a digital world

Anne Bowers and A. Rebecca Reuber

In 2013, the general manager of Hotel Quebec filed a lawsuit against a guest who had posted a review on TripAdvisor stating that he had encountered bedbugs while staying at the hotel.[1] The hotel did not dispute that there were bedbugs but argued that the incident was a one-off and claimed $95,000 for reputation damage and lost profits. Also concerned about the reputational damage caused by negative TripAdvisor reviews, a group of hoteliers in the UK discussed bringing legal action against TripAdvisor for what they regard as unfair and incorrect reviews. Unfavorable reviews can vividly emphasize disgusting elements such as smells and rats, and service providers often suspect that such reviews have been written by rivals or disgruntled ex-employees. Indeed, an executive with the France-based hotel chain Accor admitted to posting five-star reviews for Accor properties and negative reviews about rival hotels. After an investigation of such incidents, the Advertising Standards Authority in the UK ruled that TripAdvisor could no longer claim that the reviews on its website were from real travellers or were honest or trusted. The stakes are enormous for hotels: Surveys repeatedly show that the majority of people book accommodation based on online reviews.

In 2015, *Bloomberg Businessweek* made major changes to how it ranked MBA programs.[2] The new ranking algorithm favored different business schools, resulting in new winners and losers. The algorithm weighed pay, placement, and alumni metrics more heavily, reduced the weight of student satisfaction and recruiter opinion, and eliminated faculty research output as a criterion. Some schools changed by as many as twenty-five spots in the rankings, with the average change at least six spots. Deans of the losing business schools worried that the new rankings would make their schools less appealing to student applicants, donors, and recruiters, which could potentially have a reinforcing negative effect on the quality of the schools over time.

* * *

Everyone's a critic. That phrase has assumed heightened meaning as digital technologies have made it easy for people to publicly rate and review all aspects of a company and for their opinions to be readily available across the globe. From "best of" lists on magazine websites to employer reviews on Glassdoor, to product reviews on Amazon, and to service reviews on Yelp and TripAdvisor, companies are continually being judged, and those assessments have become easily accessible to everyone everywhere.

To be sure, the widespread availability of such information can help or hurt a business. After all, corporate reputation is essentially the collective judgment of the overall quality of an organization, its products, and its services,[3] and those collective judgments, which are based on people's perceptions of a company's past actions or performance, are typically used to predict its future prospects. Moreover, reputational judgments are comparative assessments, in that a company is being compared to its rivals. It's no wonder that, given the avalanche of customer feedback in the digital world, many managers have become wary, fearing the power of reviews to sway people's future choices. A recent study by Barclays,[4] however, indicates that the majority of businesses actually *benefit* from online ratings and reviews.

In this chapter, we discuss two types of online reputation ratings—curated and uncurated—and we describe the impact they can have on organizations. We then provide some guidelines for how managers can use such ratings to their advantage. Of course, the capability to harness a company's reputation ratings depends on many factors; our goal in this chapter is to point out some of the less-obvious issues that may aid managerial decision making.

curated reputation ratings

Curated ratings are produced by a third party (often a media outlet) that's considered neutral because it's not involved in transactions as either a buyer or a seller. Some curated ratings are intended to rank entire organizations against their peers. *Fortune* magazine, for example, publishes an annual list of the "World's Most Admired Companies" and the "100 Best Companies to Work For"; *Newsweek* lists the "Top Green Companies in the World"; and the *Times* publishes an annual "World University Rankings." Other curated ratings are intended to provide comparisons among products or services. CNET, for example, provides reviews of technology products; *Wine Spectator* publishes wine ratings; and *Bloomberg BusinessWeek* ranks MBA programs.

Curated reputation ratings are based on predetermined criteria for scoring organizations or their products. They are transparent in that companies know ahead of time how they will be judged, although some product quality ratings (such as for wine) may be subjective and assessed by a single individual. Changes to the rating algorithm tend to involve consultation and are widely circulated in advance. In fact, companies often need to provide data for the ratings to be determined, and their executives are often polled as experts in the assessment process. Data collection is done uniformly across companies, with new ratings appearing at set intervals, usually annually.

A high score on a curated rating is beneficial because of the perception that a neutral third party has attested to a company's worthiness, and it can position a business publicly among the very best players in its industry. This can lead to the company becoming more attractive to investors, customers, suppliers, and employees, resulting in price, cost, and selection benefits that persist over time.[5] Such a cycle of cumulating benefits is often described as one in which "the rich get richer."

On the other hand, curated reputation ratings can be damaging when a company compares unfavorably to its peers or to its own past performance. Of course, to be compared, a company must first make the list. The "World's Best Banks" list by *Global Finance* includes only the best bank from each country. In other words, the very top is visible but all other banks are not, so this list provides little reputational threat. Thus, although it's advantageous to be listed, it's not necessarily damaging to be left off, because so many banks in each country aren't included. But being omitted becomes increasingly more negative the more a company's peers are on the list. Specifically, if most peer organizations are rated or ranked, then there's a reputational loss in being left out.[6] Not surprisingly, placement in the ratings also matters. For example, the "World University Rankings" by Times Higher Education provides a ranked list of 800 universities. Differences in scores are obvious, and, even more potentially damaging, year-to-year decreases for a particular university are evident. Low scores as well as declining scores can lead to the best students and professors choosing to go elsewhere to avoid being associated with universities that have poor reputations. In this case, "the poor get poorer."

uncurated reputation ratings

Uncurated ratings are posted by people on digital platforms such as TripAdvisor, Yelp, and RateMyMD. The individuals posting the ratings are anonymous members of the general public who use the platform to communicate the quality of their direct experience with an organization, so products and service encounters tend to be rated. An organization's online reputation as determined by its uncurated ratings is therefore determined by the feedback of many people rather than by a single curator.

Typically, the content of an uncurated reputation rating is only partly structured. The structured portion tends to be numeric (for example, a scale of one to five stars), and these numbers are averaged across raters to provide an aggregate score. Because the scores are continually updated, this type of reputation rating is always in flux. In the unstructured portion, the raters write comments, which are rarely aggregated. Previous comments can get pushed to the bottom of the list and become less visible as new comments are added, sometimes leaving only the most recent comments to garner the bulk of attention.

The calculations behind uncurated ratings tend not to be disclosed, and changes are usually made without consultation or transparency.[7] Yelp, for example, takes into account the total number of reviews received by an establishment, which reviewer provided a particular submission, and whether that review has been voted as helpful, but the company doesn't reveal exactly what formula it then uses. Given the different algorithms and the lack of transparency, the impact of a one-star review (or a five-star review) on an overall restaurant rating is likely to be different across different platforms such as Yelp, TripAdvisor, and OpenTable.

Positive uncurated ratings are beneficial because people tend to trust the judgments of others. We tend to believe—and may be correct in believing[8]—in the "wisdom of crowds." In other words, better judgments are generally formed with more people participating, and digital platforms make the online ratings of hundreds and thousands of people instantly available everywhere on mobile phones, so what once might have been a difficult decision (for instance, choosing which new car to purchase) with limited information and a long search time has now become a much simpler and quicker choice supported by voluminous data. This can, however, result in herd behavior,[9] with people blindly following the decisions of earlier adopters.

Indeed, evidence suggests that the *number* of online ratings is as important a reputation signal as their average score.[10]

Although most uncurated ratings are actually quite positive,[11] they can be threatening to an organization when negative ratings and reviews are visible. In particular, fraudulent reviews, perhaps submitted by competitors, can be especially damaging because then there might not be any basis in reality to respond. Because uncurated ratings are continually updated, an isolated bad review will not be as persistently noticeable as it might be in a curated platform, which generally changes only at preset intervals. Over time (perhaps within days or even hours), isolated negative feedback will be eclipsed by more recent reviews, and a high volume of ratings is likely to smooth out extreme variations that are not reflective of most people's experience with a given product or service.

the impact of reputation ratings

Positive ratings—both curated and uncurated—can help companies gain and retain customers, partners, employees, and suppliers. In contrast, negative ratings can render developing and maintaining such relationships more difficult or costly, with serious performance consequences. That said, although the link between rating outcomes and benefits might seem direct and obvious, there are a few nuances.

First, although the general positive skew of online ratings seems beneficial, when everything is positive, the search shifts from choosing the highest rating to distinguishing among those ratings. That is, to distinguish among many five-star reviews, consumers actually have to read the reviews. Imagine a restaurant receives a negative review. If the restaurant has many positive ratings, a negative review will not affect its overall level of stars, but if people read the reviews to figure out the differences among five-star ratings, they might see that negative feedback. In fact, a negative review might be the first review they see. Research on ordering effects suggests that the most visible, first-read reviews may have an inordinately large impact on individual choice, particularly when the product being searched for is relatively inexpensive, like a meal or a movie.[12] For more costly products, such a review may be only one of many that people will read. Thus, it's not simply the rating itself but also the order of reviewer comments and the type of product or service that matters.

Second, research suggests that ratings tend to decline once they've reached the top, but not necessarily because a company begins to rest on its laurels. When a company achieves a five-star rating, it starts to attract a wide variety of customers who follow five-star ratings regardless of what is being rated. These customers may not be a good fit for the firm, and may be more likely to have unrealistic expectations. Taken together, this can translate into negative experiences and, thus, negative reviews. A recent study showed that award-winning authors saw their ratings go down after winning important prizes, not because the quality of the book had changed but because winning the prize brought in new readers who otherwise wouldn't have read the book. Those readers then rated it poorly because they were bad fits, not because of anything to do with the book quality.[13]

Finally, ratings tend to matter less to repeat customers. New customers may be apt to choose a particular firm based on its rating, but will repeat customers continually check to see if that business retains its five stars? Once customers gain experiences with a company, those experiences are more likely to have a greater influence on loyalty than are the ratings or reviews of strangers. An important caveat, however, is that repeat customers do care about ongoing ratings for status goods or services, such as luxury designer brands or college degrees from elite universities.

In addition to the above stakeholder effects, companies should consider various broader impacts of online reputation ratings. We describe five such impacts in the remainder of this section.

1. Ratings can provide valuable information about competitors. Most companies collect intelligence about their competitors, but online reputation ratings can provide much more detailed information about a larger set of rivals. Curated ratings are often calculated on the basis of information supplied by each firm, which might otherwise not be disclosed, especially for privately held businesses. Because curated ratings stack companies up against one other based on predetermined criteria, it's obvious which firms score better or worse than a particular company on, for example, customer-satisfaction indicators or investment in facilities. Although these generally are broad indicators without any nuances, the numbers can nevertheless provide useful data for an ongoing competitive analysis.

Uncurated ratings and reviews can likewise be useful. Customer feedback could, for example, reveal new information about a rival's strengths and weaknesses. Or a company could discover that the main threat to its business is coming not from its direct competitors but from firms offering substitute products whose existence is disclosed in online reviews.

2. Ratings can provide valuable information about customers. Although many consumers rely on ratings for making decisions, other sources of information that are equally powerful (if not more so) are the anecdotal experiences of friends and family. One study, for example, suggests that 83 percent of mothers and 74 percent of fathers get information about products and services from social media sites such as Facebook or Pinterest.[14] That means that the sharing that people do over these networks—including ideas, useful products, and photos of product "fails"—influences how others might feel about any particular business. Of course, a company can never collect and analyze all that information, but even if only a small fraction of these individuals is using uncurated ratings to convey their beliefs, a firm can at least obtain a sense of the overall word of mouth. This is true for many curated ratings as well. In fact, many curated raters (such as Consumer Reports and Gartner) try to mimic the experience of users when testing products, and some forms of curated ratings (educational rankings, for instance) actually do survey customers.

Moreover, uncurated reviews can provide important information that's often not revealed in other ways, and in a time frame that enables fast response. When Adobe released a comprehensive update to its Lightroom product, for example, the software had changed how users imported pictures into the program. The goal was to make the process more streamlined, but in an onslaught of negative reviews, many people howled about the loss of particular features. As a result, Adobe reverted to the original process in its next update and was able to provide current users with a workaround.[15] If the company had not seen the reviews, it might have continued evolving Lightroom, one of its most popular programs, in a way that risked alienating customers. Adobe had assumed that people wanted streamlined imports, when in fact they preferred more options. By paying attention to the reviews, the company gained an important insight about the trade-offs that users were (or were not) willing to make, and the fast response to the complaints actually led to an increase in customer loyalty.

3. Ratings can provide targeting insights. Online ratings and reviews can supplement internal data about customers to aid in segmentation and targeting decisions. Are the customers who are supplying reviews representative of a company's customer base? Are the customers who love a product similar to those who hate it? Are the best reviews from customers of a core service or from those using a new service-line extension? Answers to such questions can provide important strategic insights. One Toronto-based painting company noticed that it was receiving a significant number of estimate inquiries from people who had read its reviews on a local rating site but that it seldom landed any of those individuals as clients. The reason? Those potential customers tended to be extremely price-conscious, and the company provided high-end, large-scale services. Armed with this knowledge, the firm could change its vetting process to avoid making in-person estimates to those who were not the proper fit.

4. Negative ratings can increase trust and awareness. In certain situations, even negative reviews can be beneficial for companies. Generally speaking, having both positive and negative reviews increases trust, because consumers then feel that they are getting a more accurate set of information.[16] Thus, a firm that strives to maintain a perfect five-star rating may in fact be undermining itself because customers might believe such a score is fake. In addition, negative feedback can be valuable because knowing what doesn't work can be just as helpful as knowing what does, and research suggests that customer satisfaction increases when quality exceeds expectations, no matter what level of quality was expected.[17] In other words, a mix of negative and positive reviews can help set the appropriate expectations. Additionally, for companies that aren't well-known, negative reviews can actually increase sales because they increase awareness.[18] Although well-known companies are more likely to face declines in sales after negative reviews, if the reviews are written in an objective and accessible way (rather than as product rants), customers may still retain positive feelings about the company.[19]

5. Ratings can be industry game changers. Research on both curated ratings[20] and uncurated ratings[21] shows that both can change the rules for success in an industry. This occurs when the ratings become important to buyers and when organizations respond by changing their behavior to improve their ratings.

One important shift occurs when customers start making decisions based on reputation ratings rather than on unmeasured criteria. For example, if institutional investors decide to choose only those firms with five-star corporate governance ratings, publicly traded firms will have to consider this new dimension of competition. And when customers shift toward focusing on a rating outcome (for example, a Michelin three-star restaurant) rather than on other qualities (the presence of a renowned chef), the rating organization becomes an important third party in determining winners and losers within that industry. It should be noted that firms don't usually control the criteria that rating organizations use, and these factors can change: new ones can be added and weightings can be altered, which can affect a company's ranking, even though the firm itself might not have changed.

Eventually, organizations may start to make internal decisions based on the expected impacts of those decisions on the ratings. Research on the curated reputation rankings of law schools, for example, shows that over time, they affect internal job descriptions, admissions criteria, resource allocation, and communications strategy.[22] This is a fundamental shift from how organizations made strategic decisions in the past, and over time, the ratings criteria may become the most important factors for competition in a market, regardless of whether the industry participants believe them to be so. These criteria also become more visible, which is beneficial if they reflect areas in which a firm excels—but if they don't, all but the most highly rated firms will face an uphill battle in getting others to recognize the importance of other criteria. Furthermore, even if a company does manage to place better on the ranking criteria, those efforts may go unnoticed if others are also making improvements.

In some industries, such as the hospitality industry, both curated and uncurated ratings exist. Although curated ratings tend to favor established incumbents (such as prestigious chains), uncurated ratings (like those on TripAdvisor) tend to be quicker at recognizing the efforts of upstarts and smaller competitors.[23] Because of the resulting day-to-day volatility of such ratings, organizations may need to react more quickly to customer feedback than was previously the case.

managing reputation ratings

Perceptions of an organization's reputation tend to be driven by its product and service quality, as well as by its financial performance. In today's digital world, these perceptions are much less under the control of organizations than they used to be and are driven by the ratings and reviews of professional curators and anonymous members of the general public, yet although managers now have less control over the ratings of their organizations, they do have some discretion in managing those rankings. In this section, we describe how reputation ratings can be both proactively and reactively managed.

Proactive management: develop an explicit policy with respect to ratings. Companies need to implement an explicit policy with respect to managing reputation ratings. In doing so, it's important to recognize that the policies associated with curated ratings should be different in nature from those for uncurated ratings.

An organization can participate in multiple curated ratings and rankings. A manufacturer could, for example, be ranked in *Fortune's* "100 Best Companies to Work For," be listed in *Newsweek's* "Greenest Companies," and have its products reviewed by CNET and Amazon. Because of the sheer number of such curated ratings, managers need to determine which ones are the most important. Often, competing ratings schemes are used, so an organization might choose to participate in only those rating schemes that highlight the things it does well. For example, some business schools, including prominent ones, have declined to participate in the *Economist's* ranking of MBA programs because they dispute the methodology used.[24] Even then, managers should still pay attention to all the schemes for rankings the company participates in because the schemes could change in their power and influence over time. Indeed, before Yelp, there was Chowhound, and before Chowhound were newspapers. It's also important for managers to keep an eye out for up-and-coming curated ratings that could become influential.

In contrast, managers have no say whether a particular product or business is included in uncurated platforms. Reputation indicators are always changing, so policies need to be in place to ensure awareness of what's being said about the organization online and to enable employees to handle the unexpected in an improvisational manner. A study of British hotels reviewed on TripAdvisor, for example, found that those reviews were discussed at weekly hotel staff meetings.[25] Companies should also do more than just monitor social-media sites; they should also find ways to capture customer feedback from those sources. Some businesses accomplish this by training on-site staff to recognize and defuse situations that are likely to result in negative ratings. Other companies survey customers in order to track problematic issues before the issues result in lower ratings.

Reactive management: respond quickly to changes. Many stakeholders will know when a new curated rating comes out and will be aware of how particular organizations are positioned in that rating. As such, managers need to be able to communicate thoughtfully and fully about how an organization's placement might have changed in comparison with its rivals.

With respect to uncurated ratings, many customers who post reviews, especially those containing negative feedback, expect fast response from management. A recent study of TripAdvisor reviews indicates that after hotels start responding to negative feedback, they tend to receive a larger volume of positive reviews, and negative reviews become less frequent. The authors of that study argue that consumers are motivated to leave positive reviews when they see that a hotel appreciates the reviews left by people in the past, and that they are less likely to leave indefensible negative reviews when they are aware that the hotel scrutinizes such feedback.[26]

In sum, both curated and uncurated ratings have become useful tools for consumers in many markets, and the power of such information to drive purchasing choices may only continue to grow. As such, companies should know how those rankings work, including the less common ways in which the rankings are created and used, and companies need to develop explicit proactive policies to manage their reputation ratings. The goal is for a business to be able to use those ratings to its advantage, rather than be passively at the mercy of them.

endnotes

1. The discussion of TripAdvisor reviews is based on Barclays Corporate. (2016). The feedback economy. https://www.barclayscorporate.com/content/dam/corppublic/corporate/Documents/Industry-expertise/Feedback-Economy-Report.pdf; Hall, J. (2012). TripAdvisor banned from claiming its reviews are real. *Telegraph*, February 1, 2013. http://www.telegraph.co.uk/travel/news/Tripadvisor-banned-from-claiming-its-reviews-are-real/; Huffington Post Canada. (2013). Hotel Quebec sues Laurent Azoulay, guest, over bad TripAdvisor review, *Huffington Post Canada*, August 23, 2013. http://www.huffingtonpost.ca/2013/08/23/hotel-quebec-laurent-azoulay-bed-bugs_n_3805093.html; Morris, S. (2010). TripAdvisor could face legal action over reviews, *Guardian*, September 24, 2010. http://www.theguardian.com/travel/2010/sep/24/tripadvisor-travel-websites; and Smith, O. (2013). TripAdvisor reviewer exposed as hotel executive. *Telegraph*, May 24, 2013. http://www.telegraph.co.uk/travel/news/TripAdvisor-reviewer-exposed-as-hotel-executive/ .

2. This discussion of changes in the MBA rankings is based on J.A. Byrne. (2015). BW to change MBA ranking yet again. *Poets & Quants*, March 17, 2015. http://poetsandquants.com/2015/03/17/bw-to-change-mba-ranking-yet-again/; and IU Blooming Newsroom. (2015). Revised *Bloomberg Businessweek* rankings impact many business schools, including Kelley. http://news.indiana.edu/releases/iu/2015/10/2015-bloomberg-businessweek-mba-ranking.shtml.

3. This definition of corporate reputation is taken from C.J. Fombrun, *Reputation: Realizing Value from the Corporate Image* (Boston: Harvard Business School Press, 1996).

4. Barclays Corporate. (2016). The feedback economy. https://www.barclayscorporate.com/content/dam/corppublic/corporate/Documents/Industry-expertise/Feedback-Economy-Report.pdf.

5. See E. Fischer and A.R. Reuber, "The Good, the Bad, and the Unfamiliar: The Challenges of Reputation Formation Facing New Firms," *Entrepreneurship Theory & Practice* 31, no. 1 (2007): 53–75; and P.W. Roberts and G.R. Dowling, "Corporate Reputation and Sustained Superior Financial Performance," *Strategic Management Journal* 23, no. 12 (2002): 1077–1093.

6. E.W. Zuckerman, "The Categorical Imperative: Securities Analysts and the Illegitimacy Discount," *American Journal of Sociology* 104, no. 5 (1999): 1398–1438.

7. S.V. Scott and W.J. Orlikowski, "Reconfiguring Relations of Accountability: Materialization of Social Media in the Travel Sector," *Accounting, Organizations and Society* 37 (2012): 26–40.

8. See J. Surowiecki, *The Wisdom of Crowds* (New York: Anchor Books, 2004).

9. See A.V. Banerjee, "A Simple Model of Herd Behavior," *Quarterly Journal of Economics* 107, no. 3 (1992): 797–817; and W. Duan, B. Gu, and A.B. Whinston, "Informational Cascades and Software Adoption on the Internet: An Empirical Investigation," *MIS Quarterly* 33, no. 1 (2009): 23–48.

10. See J.A. Chevalier and D. Mayzlin, "The Effect of Word of Mouth on Sales: Online Book Reviews," *Journal of Marketing Research* 43, no. 3 (2006): 345–354.

11. See J.A. Chevalier and D. Mayzlin, "The Effect of Word of Mouth on Sales: Online Book Reviews," *Journal of Marketing Research* 43, no. 3 (2006): 345–354.

12. E. Evers, Y. Inbar, G. Loewenstein, and M. Zeelenberg, "Order Preference," SSRN, July 16, 2014. http://dx.doi.org/10.2139/ssrn.2466991.

13. B. Kovacs and A. Sharkey, "The Paradox of Publicity: How Awards Can Negatively Affect the Evaluation of Quality," *Administrative Science Quarterly* 59, no. 1 (2014): 1–33.

14. M. Duggan, A. Lenhart, C. Lampe, and N. B. Ellison. "Parents and Social Media," Pew Research, July 16, 2015. http://www.pewinternet.org/2015/07/16/parents-and-social-media/#fn-13802-1.

15. "Adobe Plans to Revert Back to Old Import Dialog," Laura Shoe's Lightroom, October 16, 2015. http://laurashoe.com/2015/10/16/adobe-plans-to-revert-back-to-old-import-dialog/; and "Lightroom

6.2 Import Update," *Lightroom Journal*, 2015. http://blogs.adobe. com/lightroomjournal/2015/10/lightroom-62-import-update.html.

16. Revoo Insight Survey, 2013. www.Reevoo.com

17. E. Anderson and M. Sullivan, "The Antecedents and Consequences of Customer Satisfaction for Firms," *Marketing Science* 12, no. 2 (1993): 125–143.

18. J. Berger, A.T. Sorensen, and S.J. Rasmussen, "Positive Effects of Negative Publicity: When Negative Reviews Increase Sales," *Marketing Science* 29, no. 5 (2010): 815–827, available at http://jonah-berger.com/wp-content/uploads/2013/02/Negative_Publicity.pdf.

19. R. Hamilton, K.D. Vohs, and A.L. McGill, "We'll Be Honest, This Won't Be the Best Article You'll Ever Read: The Use of Dispreferred Markers in Word-of-Mouth Communication," *Journal of Consumer Research* 41, no. 1 (2014): 197–212, available at http://minding-marketing.com/wp-content/uploads/2015/03/Dispreferred_Markers _JCR_2014.pdf.

20. W.N. Espeland and M. Sauder, "Rankings and Relativity: How Public Measures Recreate Social Worlds," *American Journal of Sociology* 113, no. 1 (2007): 1–40.

21. S.V. Scott and W.J. Orlikowski, "Reconfiguring Relations of Accountability: Materialization of Social Media in the Travel Sector," *Accounting, Organizations and Society* 37 (2012): 26–40.

22. W.N. Espeland and M. Sauder, "Rankings and Relativity: How Public Measures Recreate Social Worlds," *American Journal of Sociology* 113, no. 1 (2007): 1–40.

23. W.J. Orlikowski and S.V. Scott, "What Happens When Evaluation Goes Online? Exploring Apparatuses of Valuation in the Travel Sector," *Organization Science* 25, no. 3 (2014): 868–891.

24. J.A. Byrne, "More Schools Say 'No' to the *Economist*," *Poets and Quants*, October 10, 2014. http://poetsandquants.com/2014/10/10/more-schools-say-no-to-the-economist/.

25. W.J. Orlikowski and S.V. Scott, "What Happens When Evaluation Goes Online? Exploring Apparatuses of Valuation in the Travel Sector," *Organization Science* 25, no. 3 (2014): 868–891.

26. D. Proserpio and G. Zervas, "Online Reputation Management: Estimating the Impact of Management Responses on Consumer Reviews," working paper, Boston University (2015), http://papers.ssrn.com/sol3/papers.cfm?abstract_id=2521190.

6

surviving disruptive innovation

Joshua Gans

The corporate landscape is littered with the detritus of disruption. Blockbuster, Nokia, Kodak, and even the mighty Encyclopaedia Britannica, which stood strong for centuries, have all been felled by innovations that in retrospect were obvious threats but at the time were opaque in their destructive potential. Today, business leaders are very aware that disruption is possible, and boards often ask them for plans to guard against it. Unfortunately, though, far too many executives lack a thorough understanding of disruptive innovation to adequately prepare their organizations in the most effective ways.

what is disruptive innovation

To understand disruption, let's go back to the theory as it was posited by Clay Christensen in his seminal book *The Innovator's Dilemma*.[1] Christensen's goal was to understand the failure of successful companies, and he described disruption in the following way: "it arises when successful firms fail precisely because, in the face of technological change, they continue to make the choices that made them successful in the first place." Christensen identified a specific pathway by which such failures could arise. He argued that for certain types of innovations—those that initially perform worse on some dimensions but rapidly improve on others—successful firms that pay careful attention to their customers' needs may find themselves vulnerable to failure at the hands of entrants that adopt the innovations and leapfrog the incumbents in the market. What's worse is that this isn't just some blind spot. Successful firms can actually make conscious decisions to de-emphasize or seemingly ignore those innovations until it's too late. For those wanting to avoid being disrupted, Christensen had this single piece of advice: Disrupt yourself first.[2]

In this chapter, I contend that managers must think much more broadly about disruptive innovation for two reasons. First, Christensen's pathway to disruption is not the only one. I will argue that Christensen focuses entirely on the demand side and, as a result, ignores an equally important pathway that arises on the supply side. Fortunately, that supply-side pathway has been well studied (notably by Rebecca Henderson and Kim Clark[3]) and there are many lessons to learn from considering it alongside demand-side disruption. Second, there are other managerial options available than just the call to disrupt oneself (see Figure 6.1). For demand-side disruption, firms can manage disruption either by investing aggressively in the new innovation after entrants have brought it to market or by acquiring the entrants themselves. This is in addition to Christensen's approach, which calls for a firm to follow a strategy of *independence* by setting up an autonomous division to identify and commercialize innovations before entrants have a chance to do so. For the supply side, as advocated by Rebecca Henderson, firms can adopt a strategy of *integration* and ensure that their organizations are able to simultaneously develop innovations along multiple technological trajectories. The key dilemma facing business leaders, I will argue, is that they cannot do both independence and integration, which are opposing strategies.[4] Hence, leaders can choose, at most, just one of the two to partially protect themselves against disruption. They can also rely on reactive management as a defense, however. So the question is, which combination of approaches will be most effective for a particular firm?

Figure 6.1: Dealing with Disruption

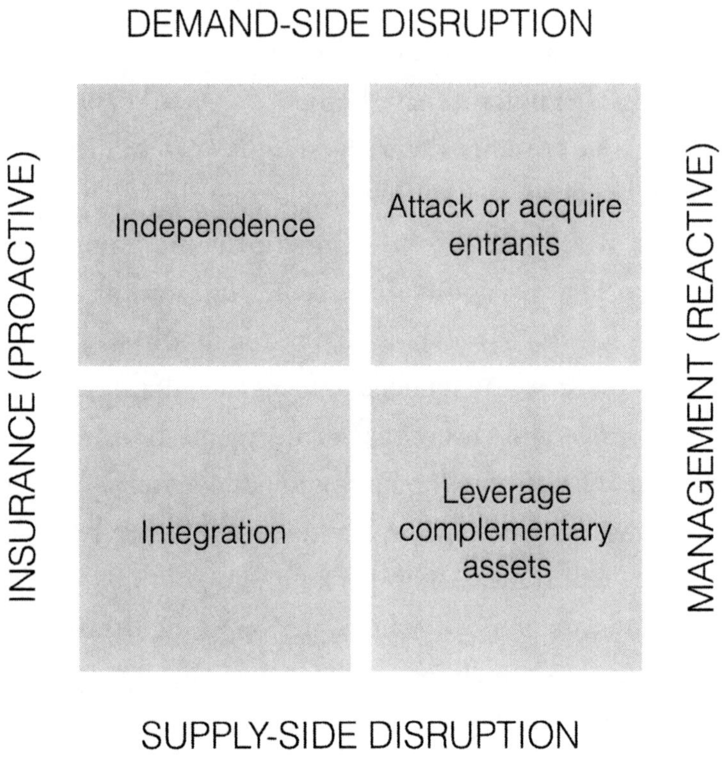

DEMAND-SIDE DISRUPTION

SUPPLY-SIDE DISRUPTION

disruption theory

Both the demand-side and supply-side theories of disruption share the belief that certain types of innovations can lead to disruption while other types do not. In each case, the innovations that can lead to disruption are ones in which the incentives and abilities of established firms to adopt the innovations quickly are muted relative to entrants. Moreover, in each case, it's hard to identify at the outset whether a particular innovation is a potential threat or will prove to be flawed in the marketplace. Thus, established firms face challenges in identifying such innovations before the fact.

For the demand-side theory, as described by Christensen, the innovations to be concerned about are those that have two characteristics. First, they tend to underperform compared to an established firm's products in serving that firm's mainstream customer needs, although they may actually be attractive to a niche segment. (That niche is often underserved by established firms, giving an opening to new entry.) Second, innovations can turn into a threat by improving rapidly along dimensions that mainstream customers care about. It's here that the threat to the established firm becomes real as entrants are able, by competing on price, to attract the established firm's marginal customers. As entrants' products improve, the competition becomes more intense and, so predicts Christensen, can leave incumbents unable to respond effectively until it is too late. That's essentially the story of how digital encyclopedias—Microsoft's Encarta and then later Wikipedia—were able to disrupt the venerable Encyclopedia Britannica. We call this the demand-side theory because the innovations that threaten incumbents are ones that do not initially appeal to current customers but end up doing so. Hence, all the action is on the demand side.

In contrast, the supply-side theory emphasizes innovation types that established firms have trouble organizing themselves to develop effectively at either low cost or high quality. According to Henderson and Clark, the way to think about these innovation types is to distinguish between two classes of knowledge that might flow through an organization and get improved on: component knowledge and architectural knowledge.

Making a product, particularly a high-tech one, requires people with specialized skills and training. No one could design and build a modern airliner on his or her own, but teams of individuals, each working on a different component of the overall system, could. To achieve that, the team employees would need to possess the necessary "component knowledge," but it's never the case that the teams can operate purely independently. At some level, knowledge must be generated that establishes how the components will be linked and how changes in one component affect the performance of others. That is, the organization must possess "architectural knowledge" that conveys how all the pieces will fit together.

Although the process by which component knowledge is acquired and improved seems quite transparent and somewhat obvious, architectural knowledge is harder to pinpoint. The best theories envision that an organization experiments at some undefined stage in its evolution with different ways of putting components together to make a product. At some point, a dominant design emerges that both manages trade-offs between components and also sets standards that should be adhered to regarding any one component's impact on others. It is important to note that this architectural knowledge is usually not codified in a way that can be communicated easily but is tacitly understood by employees.

That's the essence of the supply-side theory of disruption: Successful firms ride a set of architectural knowledge that allows the decision makers in the firm to take that knowledge as given, enabling the organization to focus on improvements in component knowledge. This is wonderfully efficient and leads to a smoothly operating business, but at the same time, there's a specter of vulnerability. What if that architectural knowledge itself becomes obsolete? What if an architectural innovation emerges?

reactive management

With demand-side disruption, an incumbent company may not know whether an entrant's innovation will be a competitive threat. When it becomes clear that the innovation is a threat, the established firm needs to respond to protect its market position.[5] One strategy is to go on the attack by aggressively investing in the new technology in hopes of controlling it as it rapidly improves on dimensions that existing customers care about. An example of this comes from Microsoft and the "browser wars," as studied by Rebecca Henderson, Tim Bresnahan, and Shane Greenstein.[6]

In the mid-1990s, the Netscape browser was taking off commercially and was launching interfaces with online applications that mimicked Microsoft's own approach with Windows. The danger was clear: Netscape could own a key complement to Windows that would not be under the control of Microsoft. In response, Bill Gates, then the CEO of Microsoft, penned an eight-page memo outlining the threat and invested in creating an entirely new division. This was no small division; it had 4,500 employees. Although Gates oversaw its strategic direction, the division was largely autonomous and was completely focused on overtaking Netscape. By 1998, it had done that, and although Microsoft has had its ups and downs since, the company remains dominant in its traditional areas of personal-computer operating systems and applications.

Another approach for reactively managing demand-side disruption is cooperating with or acquiring the disruptive new entrants. The established firm waits to see whether a start-up's innovation improves and becomes a competitive threat. Then, instead of waging war, the established firm licenses the technology or acquires the entrant and its business. My own research with coauthors Matt Marx and David Hsu has uncovered that approach to managing disruption as a feature of many markets, including our most recent study examining the start-up strategies in the automatic speech recognition (ASR) industry.[7] Over the course of more than fifty years, hundreds of firms have brought innovations into the ASR market, often under their own steam (at least initially), slowly but surely improving the technology. In our examination, we found that new entrants were indeed the first to commercialize new technologies that fit Christensen's definition of potential disruptors.

Take, for example, the start-up Vlingo Corp., which introduced a leapfrogging innovation based on grammar-free speech recognition. This was a technology that did not confine users to a set of recognizable phrases (as existing technologies at the time had required) but rather allowed them to speak freely. Not surprisingly, this was less accurate than previous technologies, but the performance improved over time. On mobile phones, this allowed users to dictate text messages rather than simply identify someone to call. Many industry incumbents, including Nokia, RIM, and Samsung, established partnerships with Vlingo, and the company was eventually acquired by ASR giant Nuance Communications in 2012.

Vlingo was hardly an isolated case. Controlling for other factors, we found that entrants with disruptive innovations were four times more likely to cooperate with incumbents than were entrants with other technologies. What this suggests is that incumbents can wait and then strike deals with the most promising entrants as a strategy to manage demand-side disruption. This makes intuitive sense, as it's precisely when those technologies have proven themselves in generating performance increases that they are a threat to established firms. Of course, established firms may have to pay more for a leapfrogging technology after it has proven itself, but they also save themselves the costs of investing in nascent innovations that do not pan out.

As difficult as it is to respond to demand-side disruption, reacting to supply-side disruption can be even tougher, because supply-side disruption cripples a firm's ability to respond. Entrants may be commercializing superior products, and internal teams may simply not be able to match that performance. In some cases, though, established firms can buy themselves a lot of time when they possess key complementary assets that entrants lack.

A great example of this emerged in Mary Tripsas's study of the typesetting industry.[8] Typesetting, of course, dates back to Johannes Gutenberg and his invention of moveable type in the 1400s, but the modern approach of using a keyboard as a primary input device arrived when Ottmar Mergenthaler invented the Linotype machine in 1886. The technology used poured liquid metal to create the type, and for decades, it was the only method of typesetting, enabling Mergenthaler Linotype, along with two other firms (Intertype and Monotype), to dominate the industry. In 1949, though, hot metal gave away to a photographic process using a xenon flash, and just over a decade later, this was done digitally using a cathode ray tube, until, finally, laser typesetting arrived in 1976. In almost every case, previous competencies were made obsolete by a new technology and established firms struggled to produce leading machines for the next generation. It was a classic issue associated with the reinvention of architectural knowledge.

The problem for new entrants, though, was that they were missing a key complementary asset, without which they could not compete with established firms. The primary customers of typesetters were newspapers and publishers, and each had a look and feel to its product that depended crucially on the font it chose. As it turned out, the vast majority of fonts were proprietary and owned by the incumbent hot-metal typesetters of which Mergenthaler was a pioneering leader. In the late nineteenth century, the company had aggressively invested in developing new fonts, building a library of 100 typefaces by the turn of the century (which grew tenfold just a decade later). Five hundred typefaces were considered a minimum number to be viable, and at Mergenthaler's aggressive rate, an entrant would need five years of continual development just to be competitive. It simply did not matter what type of machine was being used; if customers wanted Helvetica (Mergenthaler's all-time popular font), they would have to purchase it from Mergenthaler. Interestingly, Mergenthaler did not own any specific intellectual property other than the trademark on the name, but that proved enough to give the company an advantage. The dominant technology of the machines may have changed over the years, but the fonts never died.

proactive management (insurance)

Reactive management of disruption, even where possible, is costly. Consequently, savvy firms have looked for ways to insure themselves against that risk. Those who have studied both demand- and supply-side disruption have identified ways in which some companies have proactively taken actions that have helped them ride out the waves of disruption.

For demand-side disruption, the primary uncertainty that firms face is whether a poorly performing technology introduced by an entrant in a niche market may actually give rise to a trajectory of improvement that becomes a competitive threat. The idea of insuring against such demand-side disruption is this: The established firm positions itself to control that technology from the outset in case the innovation does indeed become a threat. Christensen offered a solution to the "innovator's dilemma" in the form of established firms themselves becoming the carriers of disruption. In this, he was motivated by the case of Quantum Corp.

Quantum was a significant producer of 8-inch hard-disk drives for minicomputers but did not achieve the same status in 5.25-inch drives. At the height of its first success in 1984, some engineers within Quantum saw the potential for 3.5-inch drives, especially for the emerging personal computer market, so Quantum financed the new venture—Plus Corp.—as a separate entity but retained 80 percent ownership. According to Christensen, Plus operated successfully as an independent corporation and established a market presence in 3.5-inch drives, leading that market by 1989. Prior to that, with sales of its 8-inch hard drives waning, Quantum had acquired the final 20 percent of Plus and had adopted Plus's management and organization as its own. What Christensen saw in the Quantum experience was a path by which a firm could manage disruption. To be clear, Quantum had already been subject to disruption, as it was focused on selling drives to minicomputer manufacturers, but by setting up an independent entity to explore other customer segments, Quantum was able to revive itself in a new form at a later time, thus avoiding failure. Christensen himself was unsure whether to regard Quantum as the same firm over the course of its shift from its minicomputer-to-personal computer orientation. To Quantum's shareholders, however, the decision by managers to allocate capital to the new independent venture appeared to be quite prescient.

This approach of setting up a division to invest heavily in potentially disruptive technologies is not a straightforward one. First of all, it requires true independence in decision making, lest the pressures and conflicts from the main organization encumber the division. Second, it requires support at the very top, because the new division will need resources to compete. Third, because this approach is essentially insurance, it needs to develop all potentially threatening technologies, most of which will prove to be unsuccessful; hence, it needs to be shielded from normal performance metrics. Thus, Quantum's success notwithstanding, this approach for proactively managing demand-side disruption may theoretically make sense but is very difficult to implement in practice.

For supply-side disruption, the proactive managerial (or insurance) approach is different. Although demand-side disruption involves an established firm missing a certain kind of technological opportunity, supply-side disruption arises when an established firm becomes incapable of taking advantage of a technological opportunity. Specifically, when a new competing innovation involves a distinct set of architectural knowledge, established firms that have focused on being "best in breed" in terms of component innovation may find it difficult to integrate and build on the new architecture.

The insurance premium for supply-side disruption involves reduced performance. In order for an organization to employ and "remember" architectural knowledge, those responsible for the components need to be reminded how their choices interact with the choices of others. Thus, theory implies that the firm has to be tightly integrated so important tacit knowledge can be absorbed and retained in the organization. This effort of integration can divert resources and attention away from traditional component-innovation activities and thus may reduce firm performance at any given time.

Unlike with demand-side disruption, there have been fewer opportunities to study firms that have successfully dealt with supply-side disruption. In the industry of pho-tolithographic alignment equipment (a key tool for man-ufacturing semiconductors), Rebecca Henderson identified four waves of architectural innovation that occurred in the 1970s and '80s that caused every market leader to fail. The exception was Canon, which had simultaneously invested in different generations of technology and ensured that key personnel had experience in each.[9] These investments had a long time horizon and also meant that the company often lagged others in bringing new products to market. At each step, however, this forced Canon to understand the archi-tecture of its products more deeply so employees were able to leverage knowledge in each generation to give them a foothold in the next.

The Canon experience introduces a philosophy for in-surance against supply-side disruption: Instead of exploit-ing a given architecture through specialized autonomous units innovating on components, firms might consider in-vesting in an integrated structure that embeds architectural knowledge in the minds of as many people as possible, thereby allowing that knowledge to evolve and change. This means that the organization will have a greater chance of sustainability across technological generations but is un-likely to be a leader in any one. Moreover, this approach is not necessarily a more-profitable strategy, just a distinct one. It's important to note that academic research regarding how firms can insure against supply-side disruption has not advanced much beyond this point. The case of Canon suggests the value of engaging in cross-generational research in a more or less simultaneous manner but also emphasizes the value of companies biding their time while the disruptive technology evolves. This particular feature stands in contrast to the prescriptions for insuring against demand-side disruption, which tend to emphasize urgency.

formulating an effective plan

We have now considered all of the options for managing disruption as depicted in Figure 6.1. Some of these are reactive, and we have seen that there are more feasible reactive options for managers when facing demand-side disruption than supply-side disruption. Other options are proactive, and in those cases, the emphasis is on matching the strategic choice to a particular pathway that disruptive events may play out. Figure 6.2 highlights the different examples in which firms have successfully deployed each of these strategies to manage their way through disruptive threats for long-term sustainability. As discussed earlier, however, these choices were themselves costly. Thus, business leaders will want to consider the options carefully before implementing any strategic plan for managing disruption.

Perhaps the most difficult choice is with regard to insurance. Essentially, insurance requires the payment of a premium up front for benefits that people hope they will never need. This makes it challenging for leaders to

Figure 6.2: Successful Disruption Management

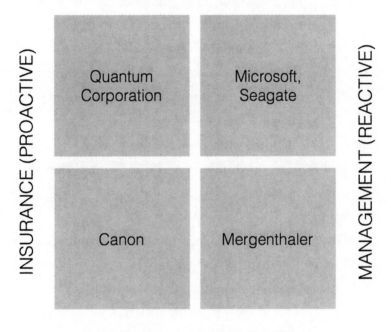

DEMAND-SIDE DISRUPTION

| | Quantum Corporation | Microsoft, Seagate |
| | Canon | Mergenthaler |

INSURANCE (PROACTIVE)

MANAGEMENT (REACTIVE)

SUPPLY-SIDE DISRUPTION

convince internal constituencies of the merits of such an approach. If that weren't enough, the prescriptions for both demand- and supply-side insurance are distinct. That is, there are no "1 + 1 = 3" synergies involved. In fact, some have argued that when it comes to the pursuit of creating an independent disruptive unit and investing in an integrated structure, 1 + 1 is actually less than 2. In other words, the two approaches are substitute strategies, and firms will be forced to choose one over the other.

To see why this is the case, recall that independence requires housing the next-generation product-development team in a separate division. Independence is about erecting barriers between divisions. A problem can arise if a new disruptive threat emerges from the supply-side, as there will be no way of providing a path by which new architectural knowledge can be integrated into the mainline business because of the barriers that have been erected. Thus, firms cannot have it both ways; they cannot pursue independence and integration simultaneously, and hence, they cannot insure against both demand- and supply-side disruption.

Given that, almost by definition, firms cannot predict whether the key disruptive event will be from the demand or supply side, what should they do to formulate a coherent strategy? In the absence of identifiable complementary assets, firms generally have more options to deploy reactive management to deal with demand-side disruption after the fact than they do with respect to supply-side disruption. This suggests that, although costly, demand-side disruption is less likely to threaten a firm's survival. Thus, if a company were to take out insurance, the sensible approach would be to focus on supply-side threats and organize the business toward deeper integration so architectural innovations can be absorbed and exploited. This is not to say, however, that managers concerned about demand-side disruption should sit idly, waiting for a crisis to manifest. Even reactive management through the deploying of resources or acquisitions relies on capabilities that can be nurtured before they are needed. That said, an effective policy for firm sustainability suggests that the emphasis should be on the proactive management of supply-side disruption. Unfortunately, this is the pathway that has usually received the least amount of attention in managerial discussions of disruption. Business leaders would do well to address that deficiency, because the very survival of their organizations may one day depend on it.

endnotes

1.   C. Christensen, *The Innovator's Dilemma* (Boston: Harvard Business School Press, 1997).
2.   The theory of disruptive technology is not without its critics. See, for example, J. Lepore, "The Disruption Machine: What the Gospel of Innovation Gets Wrong," *New Yorker* (June 23, 2014). http://www.newyorker.com/magazine/2014/06/23/the-disruption-machine
3.   R. Henderson and K. Clark, "Architectural Innovation: The Reconfiguration of Existing Product Technologies and the Failure of Established Firms," *Administrative Science Quarterly* 35, no. 1 (1990): 9–30. For a recent discussion see, J.S. Gans, "The Other Disruption," *Harvard Business Review* (March 2016): 78–85.
4.   For a comprehensive discussion, see J.S. Gans, *The Disruption Dilemma* (Cambridge, MA: MIT Press, 2016).
5.   For additional discussion of reactive management, see J.S. Gans, "Keep Calm and Manage Disruption," *Sloan Management Review* 57, no. 3 (2016): 83–95.

6.   T. Bresnahan, S. Greenstein, and R. Henderson, "Schumpeterian Competition and Diseconomies of Scope: Illustrations from the Histories of Microsoft and IBM," in J. Lerner and S. Stern, editors, *The Rate and Direction of Inventive Activity Revisited,*" (National Bureau of Economic Research: Chicago, 2013): 203-276.
7.   M. Marx, J.S. Gans, and D. Hsu, "Dynamic Commercialization Strategies for Disruptive Technologies: Evidence from the Speech Recognition Industry," *Management Science* 60, no. 12 (2014): 3103–3123.
8.   M. Tripsas, "Unraveling the Process of Creative Destruction: Complementary Assets and Incumbent Survival in the Typesetter Industry," *Strategic Management Journal* 18, no. 1 (1997): 119–142.
9.   R. Henderson, "Product Development Capability as a Strategic Weapon: Canon's Experience in the Photolithographic Alignment Equipment Industry," in *Managing Product Development*, T. Nishiguchi (ed.) (Oxford, UK: Oxford University Press, 1996): 261-279.

7

the perils of path dependence

Kevin A. Bryan

In the 1950s and 1960s, scientists in government and at some of the world's leading industrial firms, including General Electric (GE), Westinghouse, Babcock & Wilcox, Dow, and Union Carbide, worked to develop a new industry: nuclear power. Research was pursued on more than a dozen types of nuclear reactors, each of which implied different paths of future technological development, different complementary products, different regulatory regimes, and different engineer training. Direct US research subsidies via the Atomic Energy Commission (AEC) totaled nearly $40 billion (2013 dollars) during these two decades. Private-sector research, indirect subsidies, and military nuclear spending, which inevitably spilled over into civilian programs, far exceeded even that total. This lavish research spending did indeed develop commercially viable nuclear power, with worldwide capacity reaching nearly 50,000 megawatts by 1973, the majority of which was generated by a single style of nuclear plant called light-water. Despite this promising start, the nuclear industry would fade to unimportance; not a single plant broke ground in the United States between 1977 and 2013.

This outcome is surely troubling for any firm operating in an evolving technological field. Extensive research spending—on the advice of highly qualified technical minds and with incredible government support—resulted in not just failed firms but a completely collapsed industry. Worse, this collapse appears to have been at least partially the result of the industry settling on an inferior technological design. As it turns out, the light-water reactors that came to dominate the worldwide market were widely considered an inferior technology in terms of both economic efficiency and safety compared to alternative reactors that were not fully developed. The belief that light water would prove an inferior technology was held by both researchers and planners in the early 1950s, before the commercial dominance of light water was secured, and by analysts with hindsight decades later.[1]

Was this simply bad luck? In other words, were there simply unanticipated changes outside the industry that made light water less viable? Did, for example, changes in global military power, government regulation, or scientific advances make alternative technologies more lucrative? In some sense, a story of "bad luck" would not be very interesting. After all, firms always invest under uncertainty about what the future might bring, and ex-ante good investments may look bad after the fact. But this was not the case with the nuclear industry. Rather, the dominance of inferior light water, and the less-lucrative industry that followed in its wake, was foreseeable as the outcome of strategic interactions between companies that were harmful for the industry at large despite being rational for each individual firm. As such, the history of the nuclear industry holds important lessons for companies in any technologically dynamic industry and also has implications for marketing, products with network externalities, and investments in networked supply chains.

a brief history

In the early 1950s, US naval captain Hyman Rickover selected a pressurized light-water reactor as the most promising candidate for a nuclear-powered submarine largely because it was thought, on the basis of very limited technical research, to offer a quick development time. Early experience working on such light-water reactors for the navy unquestionably led GE and Westinghouse to prioritize research along those lines when developing nuclear power reactors, but there was still substantial variety in reactor types being developed by the private sector into the 1960s.

The various reactor types involved radically different design choices, with different reactors involving different coolants and moderators to sustain the nuclear reaction and transform its energy into electricity, different types of fissile material to use as fuel, different methods to control the reaction and the radiation it produced, and so on.[2] Although certain technical problems with light water had been solved while developing the nuclear submarine, even in the early 1950s, the question of which reactor type would prove most efficient and profitable in the long run was far from settled. In fact, a previously classified AEC report noted that the light-water reactor "seemed most likely to be successful in the short term, by the end of 1957, but it offered a poor long-term prospect of producing economic nuclear power."[3] In other words, the technical difficulties with generating nuclear power were least daunting for light-water plants, but inherent limits on the efficiency of those types of plants meant that they would cost more to run when compared with fully developed alternatives.

Participating utilities wanted plants with low operating costs. The problem, though, was that the government wanted plant designs that would generate useful research results. This conflict caused costs to rise rapidly and discouraged utilities from buying early demonstration plants using technologies with greater long-term promise than light water.[4] The result was a market standstill: By 1962, neither government programs nor the salesforces at reactor developers like GE and Westinghouse had persuaded utilities to purchase plants on a commercial basis.

Then, from 1963 to 1966, GE and Westinghouse began to offer turnkey contracts for fully built light-water reactors.[5] The goal was to induce lower costs via learning by doing, and the plan worked. After 1962, every nuclear plant built in the United States was ordered from one of five companies, four of which focused on light water: GE, Westinghouse, Babcock & Wilcox, and Combustion Engineering. The fifth—Gulf Oil—had hoped to usurp the existing industry leaders by developing high-temperature gas-cooled reactors, but a number of technical problems proved insoluble.[6]

Light-water reactors thereafter became quickly ensconced in the market because of increasing returns to scale. That is, as the installed base of light-water reactors grew, the unit cost of providing electricity from that technology fell, which then led to increasing sales of those reactors, thereby reinforcing the cycle of falling costs. By the mid-1970s, over 70 percent of the world's operating power reactors were light-water, with the Canadian heavy-water reactor the only alternative still commercially available.[7] Not only did costs plummet relative to other reactor types—between 1958 and just the beginning of the turnkey program, the cost of electricity generated by light-water reactors had fallen more than 80 percent—but the availability of technical support and safety information also had benefited from increasing returns to scale.[8] Nevertheless, as noted earlier, sales of light-water reactors began to dramatically slow toward the mid-1970s (even before the Three Mile Island and Chernobyl disasters). Light water, even in late stages of development, did not achieve the cost efficiency that nuclear-power optimists had hoped the industry would reach after 25 years of expensive development. With alternative reactor types receiving only a portion of the research and development given to light water, the economic failure of light-water plants ultimately led to the collapse of the nuclear power industry.

the power of dynamic increasing returns

Given this history, three questions need answered. First, why did firms initially develop light water, a technology that was unlikely to offer the best long-term mix of costs and benefits? Second, as light water began to fail commercially, why didn't firms switch to alternative reactor types? And third, how did government policy affect the behavior of firms?

An understanding of the role of dynamic increasing returns is essential to answering those three questions. According to this powerful market mechanism, the value of using a technology of type A rather than type B can grow over time depending on how many other firms or customers have used technology A or, alternatively, how much experience the firm has with that technology. The existence of dynamic increasing returns implies that relatively minor differences in conditions when technologies are new can "lock in" inferior technologies.[9]

The most famous such story is that of the Stanley Steamer. In the early twentieth century, it wasn't at all obvious that gas-powered automobiles were superior to steam-powered ones. In fact, steam-powered cars were quieter, provided a smoother ride, and handled more easily.[10] They also required water to be added roughly every thirty miles, however, and an outbreak of foot-and-mouth disease in New England in 1914 forced the closure of water troughs,[11] leading to customers temporarily shifting away from steam-powered vehicles. The result was a larger user base of gas-powered cars, which then led to more gas stations and mechanics who could work on those vehicles. This growing convenience helped increase the value of gas-powered automobiles, leading to more customers choosing them even after the water troughs had reopened. The eventual dominance of gas power, then, might have occurred even if most drivers preferred steam-powered automobiles when the installed base of each type of vehicle was identical.[12]

Note the importance of increasing returns: If the value of a car were independent of the number of similar vehicles sold, a "small event" like the closing of water troughs in New England would not have had such a huge effect. In the nuclear case, the selection of a light-water reactor for the US nuclear submarine gave GE and Westinghouse early experience in building that type of reactor, and learning by doing certainly generates increasing returns. That is, the more reactors of a given type that have been built, the easier engineers will find it to improve that technology and to build additional reactors of that type. It's important to note here that the choice made by Captain Rickover in the early 1950s was not in any way based on light water being the superior technology for the long-run development of a civilian nuclear-energy industry. As such, that decision was the sort of "small event" that can tip subsequent actions down an inferior technology path.[13]

Increasing returns—and hence the potential for lock-in—appear in many forms beyond simple learning by doing. For example, existing technologies generate a series of contracts and investments by firms upstream and downstream that remain as constraints even when an alternative technology appears to be a strict improvement. This explains the substantial difficulty that electric cars will have in usurping the dominant position of gas-powered vehicles.[14] Network effects, or the benefits of coordination on a single standard by producers or buyers, can also lock in inferior early movers.[15] In addition, "bad luck" during the early stages of research that attempts to learn about the viability of alternative research agendas in the face of uncertainty can lead to firms focusing on technologies that have a few "lucky draws" in their early development.[16] Lastly, increasing returns can result from small events that affect the development of complementary technologies for suppliers or buyers, minor differences in preferences between early and late adopters, and small gifts of luck along different research lines.

Are "small events" the only source of dynamic increasing returns that can lead an industry down a potentially inefficient path? If they were, we would again be in a situation of "bad luck," meaning there was nothing General Electric or Union Carbide could have done if Rickover's idiosyncratic choice as a military bureaucrat had locked in light-water technology. The widespread adoption of an inferior technology often occurs from dynamic increasing returns that are entirely within the control of the companies involved, however. Specifically, lock-in can inadvertently result from the *deliberate* actions of *rational* firms.

when rational actions lead to disastrous results

Why would firms take actions that deliberately lock in an inferior technology? The answer comes from the disconnect between a firm maximizing its own profits and an industry trying to maximize the profits of all its firms. Consider the following two examples.

Two firms, A and B, are competing to develop a commercial nuclear power plant. They can put their researchers to work on either a gas-graphite or a light-water demonstration plant. If firm A works on gas-graphite reactors, the research will take two years. With the demonstration plant as a model, a full-size gas-graphite plant could then be developed by both firms, with firm A's expertise in the demonstration plant enabling it to earn $6 billion and firm B to earn $3 billion. If, however, either firm works on a light-water demonstration plant, the plant can be built in only one year, after which both firms would find it in their interest to build full-scale light-water plants. In this case, the inventor of the first demonstration plant will earn $4 billion and the other firm will earn $2.5 billion. In both cases, the differential earnings reflect the relative ease of scaling up the demonstration plant by its inventor. Assume that in either case, once a demonstration plant has been built, dynamic increasing returns mean that both firms will find it most profitable to shift all of their research into scaling up that demonstration plant.

What should manager in firm A do? She will reason as follows: "If I work on the gas-graphite reactor, firm B will have its scientists develop the light-water plant, as they will finish their demonstration plant before I finish mine. And once their demonstration plant is complete, I will direct my scientists to scale up the light-water plant, earning me $2.5 billion. Alternatively, I can simply start by working on a light-water demonstration plant, giving me a roughly 50/50 shot of being first to develop it, and hence earning $4 billion for half the time, plus $2.5 billion for the other half, for an average expected profit of $3.25 billion. I am therefore going to direct my scientists to work on the light-water plant." Managers in Firm B will, of course, reason in precisely the same way, and hence both firms will work on light water even though they both accurately perceive that gas graphite would maximize industry profits.

The problem is a *strategic externality*: Once the demonstration plant for light water is built by any firm, it's no longer worth continuing development of the alternative technology. In essence, rational firms do not care that their research today affects the value of research projects initiated by rivals. That is, the effort of other firms generates increasing returns to scale that will affect the future profits of rival companies, but those other firms rationally will not take that into account.

It gets worse. Consider a second example in which the two firms can either put their scientists to work on a full-scale nuclear plant or on a demonstration plant that can be sold only in small numbers. If the full-scale plant is developed directly, the inventor earns $8 billion in the eventual market and the rival earns $1 billion, with the difference reflecting the large gap in knowledge around building full-scale plants in the early stages of a new industry. If the demonstration plant is developed first, however, the inventor earns $1 billion and the eventual market in full-scale plants will be split between both firms. In this case, the openness in development will lead to the full-scale market itself being worth $10 billion, with $5 billion going to each firm. Note that industry profits are maximized when the demonstration plant is invented first and then developed into a full-scale plant by the industry at large;

the assumption here is that it is most efficient for the industry as a whole to test things on a demonstration plant before committing to a costly full-scale plant. Assume further that because the full-scale plant is more difficult to develop, if one firm works on a full-scale plant and the other on a demonstration plant, the full-scale plant will be invented first one-third of the time and the demonstration plant will be invented first two-thirds of the time.

In this scenario, a manager in firm A will reason in the following way: "If firm B works on a demonstration plant and I work on the full-scale plant, then I will invent my plant first one-third of the time, earning $8 billion; the other two-thirds of the time, my rival will invent the demonstration plant and I can then switch my scientists to scaling up that project, earning $5 billion. The average expected profit is therefore $6 billion. If, however, I work on the demonstration plant, I will invent it before my rival half the time, earning an average expected profit of $500 million from selling demonstration plants to technologically savvy utilities, and will earn another $5 billion from developing that demonstration plant into a full-scale industry, for an overall average expected profit of $5.5 billion. So, if firm B works on a demonstration plant, I ought to work on the full-scale plant."

What if firm B works on a full-scale plant? A manager in Firm A would reason like this: "If that happens and I work on a demonstration plant, I will finish first two-thirds of the time, earning the $1 billion profit from selling that early-stage plant, and another $5 billion from helping develop that demonstration plant to scale. But one-third of the time, my rival will invent the full-scale plant before me and I will earn $1 billion. My total average expected profit is therefore $4.33 billion. If, however, I work on a full-scale plant, I will finish the full-scale plant first half the time, earning $8 billion dollars, and my rival will finish that plant first half the time, leaving me to earn $1 billion dollars, hence giving me an expected profit of $4.5 billion. Therefore, no matter what firm B does, I should work on the full-scale plant." Again, firm B will reason the same way, and hence, the industry will inefficiently develop the more difficult but less-lucrative full-scale plant. The problem is a different type of strategic externality: Rational firms do not account for the fact that their research makes possible follow-on research by rivals, and hence they care only about the profitable value of follow-on research that they can capture directly.

The lesson of these examples is that competitive firms can have incentives to endogenously introduce—that is, to create as a result of their own rational incentives—the increasing returns to scale that will lock in subpar technologies. Earlier workhorse models of path dependence[17] have described the lock-in of inferior technologies as a result of unforeseeable "small events" like the personal preferences of certain customers. But the market dynamics of increasing returns to scale can result either from the initial advantage of an inferior technology generated by small events or from the active and rational choices of competing firms! It is the latter that is worrying; unlike the cases in which industries are harmed by the idiosyncracies of Hyman Rickover or the randomness of a foot-and-mouth outbreak, firms in a growing industry can do some things to avoid the peril of a path dependence created by their own choices.

six ways to avoid path dependence

What, then, should firms in technologically dynamic industries do? The concern, of course, is that competitors may have the incentive to pursue research strategies that decrease, via path dependence, the value of the industry—or, worse lead the industry toward complete collapse. The following six lessons are worth noting.

1. Coordinate to reduce strategic incentives that lower industry profits. The fundamental cause of endogenous lock-in is increasing returns to scale at the level of the industry, combined with individual firms maximizing only their own (rather than the industry's) payoff. A gap between individual and industry-wide incentives can occur in many strategic interactions. When firms are deciding whether to undercut a rival's price, for instance, they typically don't consider how that decision might affect the rival's profits, and they might not fully realize how it could also affect the market as a whole. In the case of pricing, of course, companies are generally prohibited via antitrust laws from colluding. Antitrust laws do not, however, generally prohibit the coordination of research activity at the industry level, because more efficient R&D can benefit both consumers and firms.

Consider, for instance, a patent pool, in which firms in an industry agree to freely license patents to one another on the condition that each participant pursues a certain level of R&D. Or consider a research joint venture in which members jointly decide how much to spend on R&D and where to allocate that spending. Because firms in this patent pool or research joint venture share technology, the incentive for everyone is to choose a research portfolio that maximizes industry profit. In the late 1980s, for example, the semiconductor research consortium SEMAT-ECH[18] enabled fourteen US semiconductor companies to eliminate duplicate research spending and reduced the incentive for any individual firm to pursue research along a technological path that did not maximize industry profits.

2. Ensure that outside firms have incentives to build complements to the optimal research line. Firms should also consider inducing the development of products that are complementary to the research line that maximizes industry profits. These complements, if invented, increase the profitability for every firm in the industry to pursue the research line that maximizes industry profits as a whole. The strategy of subsidizing complements, particularly in the early stages of dynamic increasing returns, is well-known from the literature on platforms.[19] An important insight from this literature is that if complements are costly to produce, firms might consider making a credible commitment not to "step on the toes" of a complement's producer by later entering its market. Consider, for example, an online retailer like Amazon with a platform that connects buyers and sellers via a reseller marketplace. That platform benefits from the existence of third-party sellers of products that Amazon itself does not carry. These sellers, however, would be reluctant to pay the cost of sourcing unusual products and setting up Amazon sales pages unless they were sure that Amazon wouldn't undercut their business should it prove successful.

Similarly, with respect to R&D, the producers of inventions that are complementary to the research line that maximizes industry profits would be hesitant to develop those complements if they expected firms in the industry to later squeeze their margins or attempt to "invent around" their complement. In many cases, making a credible commitment to avoid such squeezes can be a huge challenge, particularly when the precise form of the complement cannot be known before it is invented. In general, industries with very few large players on the research side and with enough stability for informal agreements ("relational" contracts) to be sustained are generally better positioned to attract the complements that will help ensure that inferior technological lines are not worth pursuing.

3.   **Link internal incentives to the direct goal.** Within organizations, the actual research is performed by individuals or teams, not by the firms themselves. This means that distortions that induce harmful path dependence can exist *within* a firm for precisely the same reason that they can exist within an industry, even when the firm is a monopolist. Consider, for example, a firm that pays its scientists a bonus that's proportional to the profits generated by an invention. Moreover, assume that the firm allows its individual scientists to choose what projects to work on. Those conditions are precisely analogous to the incentive system at the industry level that was discussed earlier. Namely, individual inventors will not sufficiently consider how their research might affect the incentives of other inventors.

As it turns out, *every* innovation policy either conditions payments on the value of potential future inventions or leaves the firm vulnerable to harmful path dependence.[20] That is to say, if senior executives truly do not know which inventions are best to pursue, no "neutral" salary and bonus policy will avoid lock-in. For instance, giving bonuses to scientists for successful new products may induce them to work on too many low-value incremental inventions. On the other hand, giving bonuses to scientists only for difficult advances might encourage them to avoid incremental steps that could be necessary to develop the most profitable new technology. To walk the fine line between these two cases, a firm might consider rewarding only those breakthroughs that actually lead to the most profitable new technology, where the measure of "profitable" must adjust for the difficulty or cost of developing that technology. Ideally, a firm would initially query outside experts or perform internal data collection among the research staff to identify the optimal technological path. Then, effort along that path can be encouraged using simple bonuses for the "right" inventions.

4. Beware the difficulty of leapfrogging bad investments. Minor mistakes in the early development of a new technology can ultimately be very costly under conditions of dynamic increasing returns. Every invention can affect not only current profits but also future profit potential, depending on customer adoption, the steepness of the learning curve, and other factors. In the nuclear power industry, once dozens of light-water plants had been ordered, the technical staff had been trained, and safety regulations had been promulgated, the benefit of switching research efforts back to even a superior reactor type was very limited and hence did not occur.

In the literature on industrial organization,[21] the concept of leapfrogging helps explain some of the dynamics involved. Firms or nations with an existing product or technology (say, a developed landline network) may be slower to introduce a new product or adopt a new technology (say, cellular phones) than a firm or nation that doesn't possess the existing technology. The problem for R&D is that even experimental research may generate breakthroughs that can, because of increasing returns to scale, unintentionally place an industry on a harmful technological path. Thus, there's a danger in pursuing a research agenda that attempts to develop many technologies simultaneously. Breakthroughs in an area that's not along the profit-maximizing research path may, via returns to scale in early consumer adoption or rival follow-up inventions, lead the inventing firm to earn less profit than it would have earned had it not developed that invention at all. The desire to pursue an open research agenda—to "not put all of your eggs in one basket"—can actually be harmful!

5. Consider the distortionary effects of "free" money. In general, government subsidies — "free" money — may seem unambiguously good. If those subsidies are aimed at a technology that leads to harmful lock-in, however, the industry would clearly be better off taking a pass. More subtly, even "technologically neutral" subsidies can induce harmful lock-in. Consider the impact of a hypothetical $10 billion prize offered by the US government in 1950 for the first private-sector firm to develop a nuclear reactor attached to a power grid. Although this prize is "neutral" with respect to technology, it will shift incentives in the private-sector equilibrium toward the development of reactors that can be quickly constructed at a minimum viable scale, rather than toward reactors that are easiest to develop into commercially viable products. Once that minimally viable reactor has been developed, the difficulty of leapfrogging might then prevent the industry from ever returning to pursue what initially might have been the most promising technology. Simply put, neutral incentives do not necessarily induce neutral outcomes.

The same is true even when it comes to credit for scientific breakthroughs. Take, for instance, the development of the early airplane.[22] Worldwide fame was on the line for the first person to successfully fly a controllable powered heavier-than-air plane, and teams from as far as Australia and Brazil worked on developing a solution. The Wright brothers invented the airplane in 1903, garnering worldwide adulation, but the particular nature of their design—using wing-warping rather than ailerons for lateral control, and fabric rather than metal for the fuselage—meant that the Wright plane was substantially more difficult to develop into a viable commercial product than the planes being developed contemporaneously in Europe. In other words, the desire for scientific credit pushed the Wrights to develop an initially simpler technology that was challenging to commercialize, and hence their victory may have set back rather than encouraged the development of the commercial airplane. Consequently, firms must be aware of how "free" and "neutral" incentives such as government subsidies and scientific credit can, in fact, push an industry onto an inefficient research path.

6.   R&D is not the only investment with strategic externalities. Although this chapter has been concerned largely with endogenous path dependence in R&D, precisely the same type of analysis will potentially apply in any situation in which (1) competitive firms (2) take actions with increasing returns to scale and (3) those returns to scale are at the industry level and hence each firm's actions generate strategic externalities on other companies. Situations that naturally fit those three criteria include category demand inducement via marketing spending, sequential release of products with network externalities, and investments in networked supply chains. In each of these cases, among many others, non-coordination at the industry level can lead to lower industry profits in the long run, and these lower profits can persist even when it's known by all firms that the path pursued was suboptimal.

Would the nuclear industry have prospered had the majority of R&D and early learning by doing been directed toward reactors other than light water? That's a question best left to historians of technology, but we can safely say that the perilous path dependence that waylaid the industry—a path dependence that was foreseeable in the rational actions of competing firms—could have been avoided with savvy strategic thinking. Moreover, the lessons learned from that market collapse do not pertain only to the nuclear energy industry; in fact, they are applicable to all companies in markets governed by similar dynamics.

endnotes

1. R. Cowan, "Nuclear Power Reactors: A Study in Technological Lock-in," *Journal of Economic History* 50, no. 3 (1990): 541–567.
2. M. Hertsgaard, *Nuclear Inc.: The Men and Money Behind Nuclear Power* (New York: Pantheon Books, 1983).
3. R.G. Hewlett and J.M. Holl, *Atoms for Peace and War: 1953–1961* (Oakland, CA: University of California Press, 1989).
4. W. Allen, "Nuclear Reactors for Generating Electricity: U.S. Development from 1946 to 1963," technology report, RAND (1977).
5. W. Allen, "Nuclear Reactors for Generating Electricity: U.S. Development from 1946 to 1963," technology report, RAND (1977).
6. W.J. Nuttall, *Nuclear Renaissance: Technologies and Policies for the Future of Nuclear Power* (Boca Raton, FL: CRC Press, 2004).
7. R. Cowan, "Nuclear Power Reactors: A Study in Technological Lock-in," *Journal of Economic History* 50, no. 3 (1990): 541–567.
8. R. Cowan, "Nuclear Power Reactors: A Study in Technological Lock-in," *Journal of Economic History* 50, no. 3 (1990): 541–567.
9. W.B. Arthur, "Competing Technologies, Increasing Returns, and Lock-in by Historical Events," *Economic Journal* 99 (1989): 116–131.
10. J. Mokyr, *The Lever of Riches* (Oxford, UK: Oxford University Press, 1992).
11. C.C. McLaughlin, "The Stanley Steamer: A Study in Unsuccessful Invention," *Explorations in Entrepreneurial History* 7, no. 1 (1954).
12. W.B. Arthur, "Competing Technologies, Increasing Returns, and Lock-in by Historical Events," *Economic Journal* 99 (1989): 116–131.
13. R. Cowan, "Nuclear Power Reactors: A Study in Technological Lock-in," *Journal of Economic History* 50, no. 3 (1990): 541–567.
14. R. Cowan and S. Hulten, "Escaping Lock-in: The Case of the Electric Vehicle," *Technology and the Environment* 53, no. 1 (1996).
15. J. Farrell and G. Saloner, "Installed Base and Compatibility: Innovation, Product Preannouncements, and Predation," *American Economic Review* 76, no. 5 (1986).
16. The experience of chemical pesticides *contra* alternative forms of pest management is covered in R. Cowan and P. Gunby, "Sprayed to Death: Path Dependence, Lock-in, and Pest Control Strategies," *Economic Journal* 106 (1996): 521–542. A theoretical discussion is contained in M. Rothschild, "A Two-Armed Bandit Theory of Market Pricing," *Journal of Economic Theory* 9, no. 2 (1974).
17. See, for example, W.B. Arthur, "Competing Technologies, Increasing Returns, and Lock-in by Historical Events," *Economic Journal* 99 (1989): 116–131.

18. D.A. Irwin and P.J. Klenow, "High-tech R&D Subsidies: Estimating the Effects of Sematech," *Journal of Industrial Economics* 40, no. 3–4 (1996): 323–334.

19. See, for example, A.M. Brandenburger and B. Nalebuff, *Co-opetition* (New York: Crown, 1996); and A. Gawer and R. Henderson, "Platform Owner Entry and Innovation in Complementary Markets: Evidence from Intel," *Journal of Economics and Management Strategy* 16, no. 1 (2007).

20. K. Bryan and J. Lemus, "The Direction of Innovation," working paper (2017).

21. D. Fudenberg, R. Gilbert, and J. Stiglitz, "Preemption, Leapfrogging, and Competition in Patent Races," *European Economic Review* 22, no. 1 (1983).

22. K. Bryan, "Industrial Reversals of Fortune: The Meaning of Invention in the Early Airplane Industry," working paper (2016).

8

finding the right innovation ecosystem

Ajay Agrawal and Alberto Galasso

For several years, Abraham Heifets had worked on applying recent advancements in artificial intelligence to drug discovery. Developing a new medicine takes an average of fifteen years, and Heifets had devised a way to shrink the process to a fraction of that time using advanced machine-learning algorithms running on a supercomputer. He enthusiastically pitched his idea to all the top venture capital firms in his hometown of Toronto, but the reaction was always the same: Potential investors liked the idea, but people weren't willing to commit their capital. They wanted more-detailed business plans, requested more evidence, and demonstrated no sense of urgency. Heifets became increasingly anxious as his funds wore thin, and eventually, he realized that he had to relocate his business to Silicon

Valley, where investors would understand the potential of his idea and would be willing to get involved at an early stage.

The move proved to be a wise decision. By June 2015, Heifets's company, Atomwise, had raised $6 million in seed funding from five leading science-focused venture capital firms, and soon after, it announced collaborations with Merck, Notable Labs, and the Harvard Medical School.

The issues faced by Heifets are not uncommon among high-technology entrepreneurs during the early stages of their ventures. Without a doubt, Silicon Valley is widely celebrated as a start-up haven because of its abundance of experienced talent, capital, and experimental culture. At the same time, though, the Bay Area is also well known for its high cost of living[1] and fierce labor-market competition. Thus, buying a one-way ticket to California makes sense only if the benefits of relocating outweigh the costs. For Abraham Heifets, the move to Silicon Valley may well have saved his fledgling business; in Toronto, Atomwise might have died from a lack of funding and partnership opportunities. Given the financial and other costs of relocating, however, other high-tech entrepreneurs might be better off staying put in their hometowns. What factors, then, should people consider when making such a momentous decision?

Drawing on two decades of research in strategy, economics, and geography, we have developed a simple framework that high-tech entrepreneurs can use to inform their location strategies. The framework, which takes into account the key forces that shape regional entrepreneurial success, is useful not only for start-up companies but also for large corporations because the location decision of entrepreneurs is not only shaped by but also shapes the location decision of certain types of large businesses. Moreover, our framework has important implications for policymakers who are responsible for designing strategies to enhance the desirability of their jurisdictions.

eight crucial factors

Beginning in the mid-1990s, a large number of studies spanning diverse academic disciplines identified a variety of forces that affect entrepreneurial activity at the regional level. Our reading of this body of literature suggests that the most important regional characteristics for a vibrant entrepreneurial ecosystem can be classified into eight categories: investors, customers, suppliers, labor pool, competitors, institutions, culture, and social network. These eight factors shape the entrepreneurial success of a region by influencing the entry of new high-tech firms and by creating conditions that affect the growth of those firms. As will be discussed below, these forces are not independent of each other; entrepreneurship tends to flourish in regions scoring high across multiple factors.

1. **Investors.** For high-tech entrepreneurs, the availability of venture capital across multiple levels of investing

stages (angel, seed, Series A, and Series B) can be the difference between the success or failure of a start-up business. Investors vary in terms of their tastes for certain markets and technologies, their risk tolerance, their knowledge about specific sectors, and the other investments in their portfolio that might restrict subsequent investments because of conflicts. An ample supply of venture capitalists in a region therefore significantly enhances the probability that an entrepreneur will be able to find a good match. It should be noted that more than half of the venture-capital offices listed in the Pratt's Guide to Private Equity and Venture Capital Sources are located in three centers: Silicon Valley, Boston, and New York.[2] It's also important to remember that venture capitalists are more likely to provide funding and serve on the boards of companies that are local because geographical distance constrains their ability to monitor their portfolio companies and coach the management teams of those businesses.[3]

2. **Customers.** It's natural for new firms to start selling their products locally before expanding to national and international markets. Thus, the level and quality of local demand will influence the initial growth of a start-up. For one thing, a large local demand can lead to cost savings by allowing firms to spread their fixed costs over a larger customer base. Local customers may also provide crucial insights to develop and fine-tune a firm's products. Furthermore, sophisticated and demanding regional cus-

tomers can help a firm spot new trends and promising market segments. Often, the ongoing feedback obtained from early customers is so important that these customers play the role of development partners.[4]

3. Suppliers. Being located close to a dense network of suppliers is advantageous for a number of reasons. First, it reduces transportation costs and waiting times for inputs. CEO Jeff Bezos's decision to locate Amazon in Seattle, for example, was primarily because of the short distance from one of the largest distribution warehouses for books in the country. Second, the technological needs of a start-up are often fully understood only with frequent interaction with its suppliers. Third, the presence of multiple suppliers in one area allows the entrepreneur to shop for the best price, quality, and product fit. Lastly, some regions provide a natural advantage related to inputs for certain industries, and because office space is a key variable, an assessment of the regional real-estate market should also influence a location strategy.[5]

4. Labor pool. Start-ups must assess the presence of workers specialized in the relevant fields as well as their own ability to attract key talent to the region. Larger labor pools allow firms to find the best matches for their specialized occupations and also have an impact on the number, quality, and diffusion of entrepreneurial ideas. A variety of studies have shown that specialized workers tend to agglomerate in a limited number of locations. Very often, the supply of specialized workers is shaped by the presence of universities, hospitals, and research institutes in a region. It's important to recognize, however, that universities vary substantially in their propensity to cooperate with industry and support local entrepreneurship. One of Silicon Valley's greatest advantages is that it has a disproportionately large labor force with experience in scaling start-ups.

5. Competition. High-tech entrepreneurs must assess the competitive landscape, with special attention to other start-ups present in their region. On one hand, there are clear benefits to being insulated from competition. On the other hand, a variety of economics and management studies have shown that competition can play an important role in disciplining managers and spurring innovation.[6] When assessing a regional environment, high-tech entrepreneurs should avoid having a narrow focus and considering as competition only firms with similar products and technologies. They should also assess the nature of competition in terms of inputs, talent, and funding. Special attention should be paid to large companies present in the area, which can have a profound impact on the regional economy by stimulating the demand for new technology from start-ups and by attracting a skilled labor force. Our research has shown that innovation productivity is greater in regional environments where sizeable populations of both small and large firms coexist.[7]

6. Institutions. An effective location strategy requires careful assessment of the strengths and weaknesses of the regional economic and political institutions.[8] In particular, high-tech entrepreneurs should monitor local taxation levels, backlogs in regional courts, and trends in regional business legislation. Transport infrastructures such as airports, train stations, and roads may also have an important impact on the firm's ability to interact with customers, suppliers, investors, and competitors.

7. Culture. Picking the right location requires a good grasp of the cultural norms across different locales. Silicon Valley, for example, is known for its unique forgiving attitude toward entrepreneurs who have failed in previous ventures. Particular attention must also be paid to the local acceptance of different demographic and ethnic groups within a region, as this may influence the ease with which foreign talent may be recruited to the region.[9]

8. Social network. Individuals are embedded in local networks of social relations generated by their family, friends, and civic ties. The social capital derived from these personal relationships can be very important for entrepreneurs to raise capital and to attract employees, suppliers, and customers. This has important implications for location strategies. First, the profitability of a move to Silicon Valley is less clear when entrepreneurs have deep social networks in their home locations. Second, those regions where newcomers can quickly form and leverage social connections are more attractive than those where integration is more difficult.[10]

a tale of two regions: Toronto and Silicon Valley

As discussed earlier, Abraham Heifets had trouble raising capital for a promising technology breakthrough until he relocated his business from Toronto to the Bay Area. Other Toronto-based entrepreneurs have been able to thrive in the capital, however. Mike Serbinis, for example, was successful in raising a $25 million Series A round of funding, largely from Toronto-based investors, for his digital health platform company, LEAGUE. To better understand the crucial stay-or-relocate decisions made by entrepreneurs like Heifets and Serbinis, let's now apply the eight-factor framework to compare Toronto with Silicon Valley from the perspective of a high-tech start-up.

1. Investor comparison. The Greater Toronto Area (GTA) is roughly comparable to Silicon Valley in terms of population size, but the level of funds available for entrepreneurial businesses is much smaller. In fact, the level of venture-capital investment in the GTA is roughly one-tenth that of San Francisco and one-fifth that of Boston. Furthermore, regions with smaller pools of early-stage capital are likely to have thinner markets of investors with specialized expertise.

2. **Customer comparison.** Markets may be broadly classified as either consumer or enterprise. On the consumer side, the population of the GTA is only slightly smaller than that of the Bay Area (roughly six million compared to seven million), so for consumer-oriented products, these markets may be similarly attractive. The demographics and preferences of consumers may differ in crucial ways across these two regions, however. For example, in the case of technology products, even though Toronto is roughly the same size, many argue that the Bay Area is a more attractive market to launch in because a high fraction of its residents are early adopters who are willing to try new products and services such as ride sharing (Uber, for example), house sharing (Airbnb, for example), and on-demand valet parking (Luxe, for example).

The geographic distribution of enterprise customers is another important variable. Consider financial services. By various measures, Toronto is the second-largest financial center in North America, after New York City but ahead of Chicago, Boston, and San Francisco.[11] Not surprisingly, Toronto is home to a number of promising financial technology (fintech) start-ups such as WealthSimple. To date, however, the highest-profile start-ups in this industry are not based in Toronto but rather in Silicon Valley (PayPal and Square, for example). Even in Canada, a surprising number of prominent fintech firms are based outside of Toronto: Shopify (Ottawa), Verafin (St. Johns), Lightspeed (Montreal), Blockstream (Montreal), and Zafin (Vancouver). This hints that even though there's a much larger potential customer base for financial services in Toronto compared to the Bay Area or other regions in Canada, the financial-services companies in Toronto may not be sufficiently engaged as customers of new innovations to give fintech start-ups in the region an advantage.

3. **Supplier comparison.** Toronto has limited manufacturing of electronic products relative to the Bay Area. Furthermore, many inputs that are not available locally are imported from the United States, often involving nontrivial shipping and tariff costs. Moreover, many other inputs are imported from China. Thus, for hardware-related companies, Toronto faces a supplier disadvantage relative to Silicon Valley. In contrast, Toronto offers a greater supply of office space, which is significantly more affordable than that in Silicon Valley, and the region is attempting to capitalize on that advantage. For example, Kitchener-Waterloo in the GTA recently announced that it would build a large innovation complex specifically aimed at new hardware companies. This complex, which will exceed the size of a similar pioneer facility in Shenzhen, China, is designed to attract companies specializing in contract manufacturing, radio frequency testing and certification, and IT law.[12]

4. Labor pool comparison. Human capital either inexperienced or experienced *with respect to scaling* represents two distinct types of highly skilled labor. Inexperienced highly skilled labor is well trained and may have years of experience working at small or medium-sized enterprises. These individuals, however, have not participated in the rapid scaling of an organization. Experienced labor is not only well trained but also has participated in the rapid growth of an organization that has increased its market capitalization by, for example, one hundred times. Toronto arguably has a more attractive environment than the Bay Area for inexperienced highly skilled labor. Toronto-based talent is equally well trained yet less expensive and less likely to be poached than Silicon Valley-based counterparts, but Toronto has only a limited supply of highly skilled labor with experience in scaling, which involves growing a user base from zero to hundreds of millions of users, raising billions of dollars in equity capital, taking companies public, recruiting thousands of engineers and software developers, and outsourcing hardware manufacturing to China. Furthermore, even when Toronto-based high-tech companies do achieve product-market fit and begin to grow quickly, when compared to Silicon Valley-based start-ups, they often struggle to attract experienced talent to relocate because prospects worry that if the opportunity doesn't work out, there might be limited other attractive opportunities available in the GTA.

5. Competition comparison. Toronto is home to many large foreign tech companies, such as Cisco, Google, Uber, and Facebook, but the size and nature of their operations (predominantly sales offices) are modest and less conducive to meaningful contributions to the entrepreneurship ecosystem relative to their presence in Silicon Valley. More promisingly, General Motors recently announced plans to hire 750 people in the next two years to work on driverless cars, particularly on cold-weather features. It should be noted that start-ups in the GTA have flourished where competition has been high. For example, over the past five years, the region has emerged as a front-runner in the area of wearable technologies, led by start-ups such as Thalmic Labs, Nymi, PUSH, Muse, and Magniware, and inspired by Steve Mann, who founded the Wearable Computing Lab at the MIT Media Lab and subsequently moved to the University of Toronto (and is widely referenced as the Father of Wearable Computing).

6. Institution comparison. The Ontario government has implemented a variety of policies supporting small businesses (such as the Youth Entrepreneurship Fund and the Starter Company Program) and offers tax rates that are lower than the average of G20 countries. Moreover, tech companies also benefit from the Scientific Research & Experimental Development (SR&ED) tax credit, a Canadian innovation funding program that returns over C$3.4 billion to companies every year. In addition, Toronto has been ranked as the best city to live in North America according to the 2015 Safe Cities Index. Finally, healthcare is significantly more affordable in Canada than in the United States, especially for credit-constrained entrepreneurs. At the same time, several of the most dominant large industries in the GTA are heavily regulated and thus protected from global competition (for example, banking, insurance, and telecommunications). As a result, these industries do not seem to foster technology entrepreneurship at a level commensurate with their size. Thus, start-ups in these regulated industries are significantly more prolific in the Bay Area, despite there being fewer established firms from those industries in that region.

7. **Culture comparison.** Like the Bay Area, Toronto is well connected to other prominent metropolitan areas in North America, given its geographical location and its large international airport. Overall, Toronto has a vibrant, creative community and a number of strong engineering and science programs linked to educational institutions (such as the University of Toronto and the University of Waterloo) that are similar on most important dimensions to those in the Bay Area (such as UC Berkeley and Stanford). Given that foundation, it's not surprising that the GTA has a healthy concentration of technology talent: About 55 percent of technology workers in Ontario and about 26 percent of all technology workers in Canada are employed in Toronto.[13] Although Toronto has a vibrant and growing

technology entrepreneurship community, the dominance of this culture does not compare to that in Silicon Valley. The executive director of C100, an association for Canadian entrepreneurs in San Francisco, recently had this to say: "Tech is everywhere here [in Silicon Valley]. It's in the coffee shops, it's on street corners, it's in restaurants, it's in everyone's conversations."[14] This reflects not only the density of the technology-oriented labor market in the Bay Area but also a cultural mindset regarding risk taking, work ethic, growth aspirations, and other characteristics.

8. **Social network comparison**. A strong local social network is one of the most likely reasons for an entrepreneur to stay at home rather than move. One widely referenced characterization of entrepreneurship, coined by Howard Stevenson of the Harvard Business School, is this: "the relentless pursuit of opportunity without regard to resources currently under control." Entrepreneurs leverage every asset they have in their pursuit of opportunity. For those with a wide and valuable local social network, this becomes an important asset to leverage for access to capital, key recruits, customers, suppliers, regulators, and so on. Although Silicon Valley is well known as an open community where outsiders are able to establish social networks over time, such establishment still takes effort and resources and thus may be relatively costly for individuals who already have strong social networks at home.

advice for high-tech entrepreneurs

The eight-factor framework discussed in this chapter indicates the key issues that high-tech entrepreneurs must examine to assess the desirability of potential locations for their start-ups. In deploying that framework, entrepreneurs should also consider the following.

There is no universal "best" strategy. The effects of a relocation will differ across various start-ups. To assess those effects, entrepreneurs should use a two-step process when evaluating the framework presented in this chapter. First, they should assess how important each of the eight factors is for their venture. For example, cash-starved start-ups like Atomwise should give a much larger weight to investors than to suppliers. In contrast, start-ups that have secured capital and aim to scale up quickly should give large weights to suppliers and labor pools. The second step is to contrast the local ecosystem with the new location by focusing on the key factors that were identified in the first step. Relocating is likely to be the right strategy for a venture only if the new location significantly outperforms the local region for the most salient factors.

Mispriced factors can undermine the analysis. Picking a location is a key strategic decision that has a long-term impact and is difficult to reverse. It is thus crucial to price correctly the factors affecting the location strategy. Some entrepreneurs overestimate the costs (both monetary and nonmonetary) of moving and treat their business sites as cast in stone, while others underestimate those same costs. Particular attention should be paid to the value of a local social network, which is one of the most likely reasons for an entrepreneur to stay at home rather than move. For example, although Silicon Valley is well known as an open community where outsiders are able to establish social networks over time, establishing a network takes effort and resources and thus may be particularly expensive for individuals who already have strong social networks at home. Such was the case at Nymi, a Toronto-based start-up producing wearable devices that deliver biometrically secured authentication. A strong local network gave Nymi an advantage in building a team and in obtaining early seed-stage funding. Doing the same outside Toronto would have been much harder and would have required the firm to divert more time and resources away from its core business.[15]

The right innovation ecosystem can change over time. A start-up that moves may find at a later stage that it makes better sense to return to its home location. Take, for example, Taplytics, a Toronto start-up specializing in A/B testing. The company had previously relocated to the Bay Area because at that time, the founding team wanted to be close to Silicon Valley's network of investors, competitors, and customers. As time passed, however, Taplytics' products started gaining traction with a number of prominent corporate clients located elsewhere, including Target,

Indigo, and the Globe and Mail. Management then realized that the benefits of being physically located in California had decreased and that relocating to Toronto could
substantially increase the firm's profits because of the lower
tax rates and cost of talent.

**Strengths of the local ecosystem should not be
overlooked.** The eight-factor framework not only is useful
for deciding whether to leave a location but also can help
entrepreneurs identify the strengths of their local ecosystems and develop strategies that leverage those regional advantages. For example, start-ups could identify areas in
which local universities display research excellence, and
then use that valuable information to improve their recruiting and product-development strategies.

**Stay and leave are extremes along a continuum of
possibilities.** Entrepreneurs may also consider straddling
their home cities and new locations, perhaps through frequent travel between the two sites, the temporary rental of
office spaces, or the opening of a permanent satellite office.
For instance, Karl Martin, the founder of Toronto-based
Nymi, flies to Silicon Valley every six to eight weeks to
meet with his US investors. Venture-capital firms may also
provide different mechanisms for straddling two locations.
For example, the California-based accelerator 500 Start-
ups offers a program that allows selected start-ups to con-
nect with mentors and industry experts in Silicon Valley

without leaving their home locations.

policy implications

The framework also provides important insights to policymakers aiming to enhance the economic desirability of their jurisdictions. In developing policies to spur local innovation and to attract and retain talent, the following need to be considered.

Effective regional policies should target multiple aspects of the local economic environment. Focusing exclusively on only one factor may not be as effective as a multifactor approach. In other words, exploiting just one policy lever (for example, attracting high-skill workers) could help spur some business growth, but not nearly as much as would the implementation of a mix of policies (reducing taxes to new firms, investing in the transportation infrastructure, funding local arts organizations, and so on).

There is no universal "best" policy. Rather, the optimal policy depends on the economic and social conditions of the region at a given time. For example, a region with a vibrant capital market but without a large pool of talent may benefit more from policies designed to incentivize the activities of universities and research centers rather than from policies aimed to attract more investors.

Conversely, a region with a strong research environment but without a substantial presence of venture capital may benefit most from policies that help attract investors.

lessons for CEOs of large firms

The eight-factor analysis is also useful for the CEOs of global corporations. That's because the location decision for entrepreneurs is not only shaped by but also shapes the location decisions of large firms. For example, Boston's thriving start-up ecosystem was a crucial factor behind the recent move of General Electric from Connecticut to Boston. As CEO Jeffrey Immelt said in a statement, GE wanted "to be at the center of an ecosystem that shares our [GE's] aspirations." Similarly, GM recently announced that it would expand its presence in Canada, attempting to attract Canadians back from Silicon Valley, primarily to work in the province of Ontario. The plan is to hire 750 people in the next two years to work on driverless cars, particularly on the cold-weather features of those vehicles. GM selected Canada for the expansion "because of its clear capacity for innovation, proven talent, and strong ecosystem of great universities, start-ups, and innovative suppliers."

Local high-tech entrepreneurs can profoundly affect large firms' profitability. First, large companies may be especially well positioned to exploit innovations generated by local high-tech start-ups, not only as customers but also as acquirers. For example, in the area of artificial intelligence, Salesforce acquired Palo Alto's MetaMind for about $30 million, GM acquired San Francisco's Cruise for more than $1 billion, and Google acquired London-based DeepMind for more than $500 million. In addition, technology start-ups are often an important source of talent for large companies. It's important to note, however, that the flow will generally be in both directions, as specialized high-skill workers are likely to behave differently when large and small firms coexist. Specifically, our research has shown that employees of large firms are more likely to leave their companies and become entrepreneurs when a large number of high-tech start-ups are present in the region. This is because the presence of many small firms generates a thick local input market and spurs a culture of entrepreneurship that lowers the risks and costs of starting new entrepreneurial ventures.

Ecosystems evolve dynamically. In using the eight-factor framework to assess an ecosystem, CEOs of large corporations should consider not only the current levels but also the trends in the economic forces underlying the various factors. For example, the population of the metropolitan area of Austin, Texas, is currently experiencing very fast growth (annual increase of 3 percent) and is expected to soon exceed three million people. In such a dynamic environment, the numbers and characteristics of consumers, suppliers, and specialized workers are likely to change considerably, as will the characteristics of the supporting infrastructure.

Ecosystems can be shaped. The eight-factor model can provide corporate CEOs with guidance on how to invest in their ecosystems in ways that will increase their organizations' competitive advantages. In February 2015, for example, Uber announced a strategic partnership with Carnegie Mellon University in Pittsburgh to develop a leading cluster of experts in driverless-car technology. Similarly, Google has shaped the Toronto-Waterloo regional ecosystem by investing in organizations such as Communitech and the University of Waterloo.

The eight-factor framework presented in this chapter indicates the key issues that high-tech entrepreneurs must examine to assess the desirability of potential locations for their new ventures. Decades of research on innovation ecosystems and entrepreneurship have shown that these factors are particularly important determinants of a thriving regional environment. Ignoring them may lead founders to pick the wrong locations, resulting in potential difficulties in attracting the necessary funding, talent, suppliers, partnerships, and customers. Assessing them properly will lead to the best location choices, however, setting the stage for their start-ups to flourish instead of wither.

endnotes

1. In early 2016, the Palo Alto City Council voted to study a proposal that would essentially subsidize new housing for families earning less than $250,000, an upper limit that would place such a family approximately in the top 2 percent of the overall income distribution in the United States. See http://sanfrancisco.cbslocal.com/2016/03/22/250k-per-year-salary-could-qualify-for-subsidized-housing-under-new-palo-alto-plan/.)

2. Also see R. Florida and K. King, "Rise of the Global Startup City: The Geography of Venture Capital Investment in Cities and Metros across the Globe," report published by Martin Prosperity Institute (2016).

3. S. Samila and O. Sorenson, "Venture Capital, Entrepreneurship, and Economic Growth," *Review of Economics and Statistics* 93, no. 1 (2011): 338–349. See also J. Lerner, "Venture Capitalists and the Oversight of Private Firms," *Journal of Finance* 50, no. 1 (1995): 301–318; and H. Chen, P. Gompers, A. Kovner, and J. Lerner, "Buy Local? The Geography of Venture Capital," *Journal of Urban Economics* 67, no. 1 (2010): 90–102.

4. A. Bhide, *The Venturesome Economy: How Innovation Sustains Prosperity in a More Connected World* (Princeton, NJ: Princeton University Press, 2008).

5. A. Saxenian, *Regional Advantage* (Cambridge, MA: Harvard University Press, 1996); and A.L. Saxenian, "Beyond Boundaries: Open Labor Markets and Learning in Silicon Valley," in M.B. Arthur and D.M. Rousseau, editors, *The Boundaryless Career: A New Employment Principle for a New Organizational Era* (Oxford, UK: Oxford University Press, 1996): 23–39. See also E.L. Glaeser and W.R. Kerr, "Local Industrial Conditions and Entrepreneurship: How Much of the Spatial Distribution Can We Explain?" *Journal of Economics & Management Strategy* 18, no. 3 (2009): 623–663; and R.W. Helsley and W.C. Strange, "Matching and Agglomeration Economies in a System of Cities," *Regional Science and Urban Economics* 20, no. 2 (1990): 189–212.

6. P. Aghion, N. Bloom, R. Blundell, R. Griffith, and P. Howitt, "Competition and Innovation: An Inverted-U Relationship," *Quarterly Journal of Economics* 120, no. 2 (2005): 701–728. See also N. Bloom and J. Van Reenen, "Measuring and Explaining Management Practices Across Firms and Countries," *Quarterly Journal of Economics* 122, no. 4 (2007): 1351–1408.

7. A. Agrawal and I. Cockburn, "The Anchor Tenant Hypothesis: Exploring the Role of Large, Local, R&D-Intensive Firms in Regional

Innovation Systems," *International Journal of Industrial Organization* 21 (2003): 1227–1253. See also A. Agrawal, I. Cockburn, A. Galasso, and A. Oettl, "Why Are Some Regions More Innovative than Others? The Role of Small Firms in the Presence of Large Labs," *Journal of Urban Economics* 81 (2014): 149–165; and M.E. Porter and S. Stern, "Innovation: Location Matters," *MIT Sloan Management Review* 42, no. 4 (2001): 28.

8. D. Acemoglu, S. Johnson, and J.A. Robinson, "Institutions as a Fundamental Cause of Long-Run Growth," *Handbook of Economic Growth* 1 (2005): 385–472. See also A. Agrawal, A. Galasso, and A. Oettl, "Roads and Innovation," *Review of Economics and Statistics*, forthcoming in 2016.

9. A. Agrawal, D. Kapur, and J. McHale, "How Do Spatial and Social Proximity Influence Knowledge Flows? Evidence from Patent Data," *Journal of Urban Economics* 64 (2008): 258–269.

10. See O. Sorenson and P.G. Audia, "The Social Structure of Entrepreneurial Activity: Geographic Concentration of Footwear Production in the United States, 1940–1989," *American Journal of Sociology* 106, no. 2 (2000): 424–462. See also E. Damiano, H. Li, and W. Suen, "First in Village or Second in Rome?" *International Economic Review* 51 (2010): 263–288.

11. Daniel Tencer (2015) "World's Top Financial Centres: Toronto Now in The Top 10," Huffington Post Canada, September 24th, http://www.huffingtonpost.ca/2015/09/24/toronto-global-financial-centre_n_8188916.html.

12. Karen Ho (2016) "Massive innovation complex coming to Kitchener-Waterloo" the Globe and Mail, June 21, http://www.theglobeandmail.com/report-on-business/small-business/startups/massive-innovation-complex-coming-to-kitchener-waterloo/article30543400/.

13. City of Toronto (2015) "From Concept to Commercialization: A Startup Eco-system Strategy for the City of Toronto," feasibility study, http://www.toronto.ca/legdocs/mmis/2015/ed/bgrd/backgroundfile-78748.pdf.

14. Tracey Lindemann (2015) "Dear Canadian entrepreneurs: Silicon Valley wants you to stay home" November 16, http://www.theglobeandmail.com/report-on-business/small-business/sb-growth/dear-canadian-entrepreneurs-silicon-valley-wants-you-to-stay-home/article26928096/.

15. Karl Martin (2015) "Here's What Can Happen When a Startup Stays out of Silicon Valley" Fortune online commentary, November 27, http://fortune.com/2015/11/27/startups-silicon-valley-investors/.

9

avoiding implementation traps

Will Mitchell

In the early 1990s, Eli Lilly was struggling to survive. The drug giant had just one major growth product—the antidepressant Prozac—despite spending more than 15 percent of sales on R&D, and the firm's profitability had fallen to 7 percent return on sales, about half the industry average. Founded in 1876, Eli Lilly had a proud history as a pharmaceutical innovator in areas such as insulin, penicillin, and neurology, but the company found itself at risk of being acquired by a stronger competitor. What had happened?

the implementation trap

The core of Eli Lilly's problems was deadly: The company had fallen into an implementation trap, a common syndrome in which companies try to grow by focusing on the efficient execution of their existing strategies and operations even though the business environment around them has transformed. Implementation traps take multiple forms. Some companies continue to emphasize internal development despite the fact that technology and markets have shifted away from their historic strengths. Others depend primarily on partnerships to obtain new resources, neglecting to create an internal base of skills. Still others rely too heavily on acquisitions and are left with the difficulty of having to integrate an unwieldy hodgepodge of products and services. In Eli Lilly's case, management had relied heavily on internal R&D to fuel the development of new drugs, a strategy that had worked for decades but had now left the company vulnerable with an uncertain pipeline of products.

The fundamental issue here is that firms often fail to consider new ways to obtain the resources they need, and when their attempts to grow falter, the common response is simply to try harder with their current approach, which may no longer be effective. Thus, they fall into the implementation trap, doggedly trying to perfect the wrong course of action. Such one-trick ponies continue refining what they've come to believe are best practices carefully developed through learning-by-doing, repetition, and training when instead they should be developing new modes of growth. It is hugely tempting to repeat what has worked in the past, yet the implementation trap is an existential snare. Simply put, implementation excellence will not guarantee success—and in fact might even lead to failure—when a company has made the wrong choices of which growth modes to implement.

Several studies reinforce that conclusion. For example, in our research on 150 telecom companies during the transformation from analog to digital technology and from regional to global markets, we found that firms that had learned to use multiple growth modes outperformed those that emphasized a single approach.[1] Indeed, firms that used multiple modes were more than 10 percent more likely to survive five years into the future than those that focused on internal development, almost 50 percent more likely than those using only alliances, and more than 25 percent more likely than those relying on just acquisitions. Similarly, research in the life-sciences sector found that companies that mixed internal development and acquisitions were much more successful in introducing new products than were those that emphasized a single sourcing mode.[2]

Unfortunately, many firms struggle to develop balanced portfolios for resource sourcing. In our research, studying companies in the telecommunications, life-sciences, and other sectors,[3] we identified five warning signs that a firm might be falling into an implementation trap:

1. Implementation is key: Employees believe that success depends on working hard with one key growth mode and repeating it in new projects.

2. We do it best: Employees believe there's no need to seek external help.

3. Everyone else knows more than we do: Employees quickly discount internal capabilities in favor of external skills and expertise.

4. Mergers and Acquisitions are the answer: Employees have a "buying spree" mentality and M&A teams are rewarded for making deals rather than for seeing those deals through to success.

5. Corporate development rules the roost: Employees who lead the acquisitions strategy dominate external sourcing, followed by others involved in licensing and alliances, leaving those responsible for internal development feeling undervalued.

These signs are indications of potential trouble, but they do not necessarily spell disaster. In fact, our research has identified effective strategies of a multimodal approach that firms can use to avoid becoming stuck in an implementation trap.

developing a multimodal approach: build, borrow, and buy

The core idea of a multimodal approach is that companies benefit by using a mix of internal development (build), focused partnerships (borrow), and business acquisitions (buy) when they seek the resources needed to pursue strategic opportunities (see Figure 9.1). Without this balanced approach of build, borrow, and buy (BBB), firms often fall into an implementation trap, working excessively hard to create new products and services through their traditional modes of growth.[4] To avoid that trap, the BBB approach provides five rules that can help firms select how best to obtain the resources they need.[5]

Rule 1: Build. Exploit your relevant base, but don't overestimate the relevance of your internal resources. If you possess skills that are relevant to the challenges and opportunities you face, by all means, develop new resources internally. Internal development is often faster, more nuanced, and easier to protect than external sourcing. Indeed, your first question when you face a gap in the resources you need to achieve a strategic goal should typically be "Can we do it internally—quickly enough and well enough compared to our competitors—to lead our market?"

Here, companies need to be clear-minded about whether existing skills really are strong enough to get to market successfully. Firms often grossly underestimate the gap between the skills they possess and those they need, and they often fail to recognize the difficulties of conducting internal projects. Sometimes, the gap arises because the new skills require technological and market understandings that are very different from a firm's existing skill set. Other times, the new skills may seem to be similar to an existing base yet require very different systems and structures to develop successfully, thus risking strong pushback from the current organizational power bases.

In either case, whether the technical skills or the organizational requirements are too different, internal projects will often falter. Many established European telecom firms fell into that trap in the late 1990s, when they began to move into the data-networking environment.[6] Several of those early moves failed because the companies had overly relied on their traditional in-house skills and development processes, only to find that those internal capabilities were too slow to adapt to the new digital technologies. Others encountered substantial conflict with entrenched regional organizations that resented and resisted the shift of resources to the new initiatives. Eventually, many companies found that they needed to use alliances and acquisitions to complement their internal R&D. For more than a few of those businesses, that realization came too late and they were acquired by competitors.

Rule 2: Borrow. Learn to use contracts and alliances to obtain new resources. Once firms realize that internal development will not suit a particular opportunity,

Figure 9.1: Strategic Resource Gap

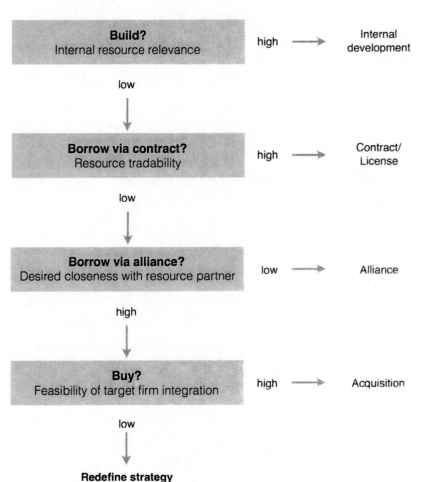

they must consider what kind of external growth mode to use. The options are to borrow via a basic contract or alliance, or to buy via an acquisition. Many firms skip over the borrowing options and jump straight to acquisitions. They might see M&As as a convenient shortcut to achieve growth, they could have an excessive need for full control, or they might simply be caught up in the excitement of a deal. M&As can waste time and money, and they risk disrupting a business because of the integration effort required. Moreover, jumping too quickly to acquisitions can cause firms to miss opportunities to learn from independent partners—often with more flexibility and lower costs than M&As.

If internal development is not feasible, then you should first consider partnerships, whether through basic contracts or more hands-on alliances. Basic contracts will be appropriate when the resources and the working relationships you need from your resource partner can be defined clearly and you believe you can defend the terms of an agreement. Given both these conditions, resources become "tradable" and success is often achievable. Through a basic contracting strategy, you can obtain resources without incurring the costs of a more complex alliance or of integrating a full organization though an acquisition. According to research in the global aerospace industry, contracting may be most successful when companies also have strong internal capabilities that will help them absorb new knowledge.[7]

If a basic contract is not viable, either because an agreement would be ambiguous or you have concerns about protecting your proprietary rights, the next option is to consider more complex alliances. These are more-involved partnerships that help facilitate collaborative resource sharing. Alliances also need to be supported by contracts, but here, the agreements tend to involve more contingencies about the evolving state of products and markets.

Alliances have the greatest chance of success when both of two conditions hold. First, you and your partner have goals for the deal that are aligned. This will help minimize conflict as the partnership proceeds. Second, the scope of collaboration with your partner involves a limited number of points of contact. This will enable a smoother ongoing coordination between the different parties.

Borrowing strategies via basic contracts or hands-on alliances can be an effective mode for obtaining resources that you can't develop internally. In some cases, though, you might not be able to write a clear contract, you cannot align your goals, or you would need to develop such a complicated partnership to manage the necessary activities that the relationship will fail. If so, then it's time to consider a full acquisition.

Rule 3: Buy. Acquisitions are important, but they are the last resort, not the first choice. Acquisitions are powerful tools that can be key to fundamental business change.[8] Indeed, acquisitions ultimately become necessary for almost all firms that seek to flourish and survive over time, yet businesses often struggle to achieve the value they expect from their acquisitions. The common diagnosis is that the post-acquisition integration was flawed, and the prescription is that the firm should work harder to integrate its next target. Unfortunately, that advice often only reinforces the implementation trap. Rather than simply working harder on post-acquisition integration, firms need to step back and ask whether acquisitions are the best mode to obtain the resources they need.

Acquisitions can be the best solution when centralized control will help a firm exploit the combined resources more deeply than could be achieved with an alliance, even through a complex collaboration. Acquisitions require many steps to exploit their full value, however. Too often, firms get swept up in the potential of a deal and fail to lay the groundwork for how they will make the acquisition work—until it's too late and they discover that the deal never should have occurred in the first place or they start down a flawed integration path before fully considering other, better, routes.

Before acquiring any business, you should perform two steps. First, have clear milestones for the integration pathway *before* deciding to complete a deal. Negotiating deals is fun. By contrast, thinking about how to make them work is often ambiguous, time consuming, and contentious, yet identifying a viable path is essential to deciding whether to complete a deal. This doesn't mean that knowing every step is required—unexpected discoveries will inevitably occur along the way—but it does mean having a clear goal for what you want to accomplish with the acquisition, what the major stages will be for accomplishing the goal, and who will need to be involved as the stages unfold. Without that crucial information, undertaking the deal will likely be a mistake—a mistake that could be severe enough to put the fate of your firm at risk.

Second, you need to understand the incentives and motivations of the people whom you'll need to carry out the integration. It's not enough simply to know who will be involved; you also need credible belief that they will be willing to stay and do the work. Key individuals from target companies often leave because they don't believe they will be valued in the combined organization, and people from the acquiring firm frequently quit because they fear the disruptions that will occur during integration. With that in mind, you need to identify and engage with the key integration leaders from both the target and the buyer, and be sure that you can provide the right incentives for them. Otherwise, the deal will likely fail.

Even experienced acquirers struggle with these tasks, and that's why companies like Cisco, General Electric, and Johnson & Johnson have developed templates that fit common types of acquisitions.[9] Those templates, however, do not negate the need for acquirers to adapt their practices. In a deep sense, post-acquisition integration is more job-shop adaptation than assembly-line automation. If you can lay out the integration stages in a way that key people will embrace—even if you can't identify every incremental step, you need to specify the major way stations along the route—the acquisition will stand a much better chance of success. If you can't lay out a viable path, then even a seemingly invaluable deal will waste your time and money, and possibly kill your firm.

Rule 4: Divest. Get rid of what you no longer need, while it's still valuable. Just as adding required resources is important, so is eliminating unnecessary ones. Firms that grow without divesting can become slow and unwieldy. I stress that divestiture is not necessarily a sign of failure; instead, divestiture is important for remaining successful. Indeed, past research by Elena Vidal and myself has shown that the most active divesters in the global pharmaceutical industry aren't struggling but instead are high performers. [10] In addition, our current research project suggests that an active divestiture strategy helps successful firms continue to grow and build their profitability.

Divestiture may be appropriate for at least two reasons. First, some ventures—whether based on internal development, alliances, or acquisitions—turn out to be mistakes. Rather than double down on errors, consider selling them to other firms that can better utilize their assets. Second, other ventures might have been highly valuable in the past but are no longer central to future growth, even if they retain substantial value. Instead of waiting for their value to decline, it's often best to sell them while they can command a strong price. In either case, divesting the resources will gain money and, at least equally importantly, free up time and attention to invest in new, higher-potential opportunities.

Most centrally, divestiture can be crucial to ongoing business reconfiguration.[11] Some divestitures involve shedding full business units, leaving a more streamlined corporate framework. Others consist of selling off product lines, often while integrating remaining lines with other units. Such complex reconfigurations can be key not just to streamlining the organization but also to more overarching corporate retargeting as technologies, markets, and environments change.

Rule 5: Pivot. Revisit your strategy when the options you have considered so far won't work. Figure 9.1 provides a pathway that begins with considering internal development, moves through contracts and alliances, and concludes with acquisitions. This approach strongly suggests that acquisition is the mode of last resort, to be reserved for cases that do not suit any other path; however, that doesn't mean that you should undertake an acquisition simply because you've rejected the other growth modes. If an acquisition doesn't appear to make sense, because either a relevant target is not available or you cannot identify a viable integration pathway, you may be able to revisit a somewhat more complex version of the options you rejected earlier. You might, for example, consider setting up a semi-independent business unit to explore a new opportunity, or investigate establishing a more complex version of an alliance that you previously rejected.

Rather than stubbornly sticking with your original growth objective, though, you might be better off returning to square one. That is, if you can't identify a viable route to your original goal, then step back, revisit your strategy, and consider other goals. Other strategic opportunities almost always exist, and they may even offer superior targets for growth. Quite simply, it's better to change destinations than to destroy your firm by trying to reach a hopeless target.

practicing the BBB approach

As early as possible, firms should experiment with multiple modes of growth, ideally from positions of strength before rigid traditions and reliance on a single mode start to hurt their performance. As part of that process, companies could develop certain goals that specifically help them learn the skills of selecting and using multiple sourcing options. In the best strategic worlds, they should undertake this experimentation before the organization evolves into a one-trick pony and becomes obsolete in a dynamic market.

Yet, we know that companies tend to form inflexible habits. Entrenched groups and leaders generate resistance. Internal staff members overestimate the strength of their current skills relative to the competitive frontier and have a hard time accepting the value of external resources. Licensing staff might be blind to the value of a more complex partnership. And powerful M&A teams do not want to consider turning a potential deal into an alliance. Moreover, the personal preferences of the top management team can complicate thoughtful decision making. Some senior executives have the souls of inventors, leading them to demand what they believe is the integrity of internal organic growth, while others are compulsive shoppers and use their love of deal making to expand their firms. To succeed, however, leaders must learn how to identify the best ways to help their companies change and grow, even when some choices may mean shifting away from their personal preferences and the strategies that may have been effective in the past. In doing so, they will help build the discipline within their organizations to choose and deploy the different modes of growth.

the resurgence of Eli Lilly

To appreciate the power of the BBB framework, let's return to Eli Lilly. As we saw earlier, the company was struggling in the early 1990s, leaving it vulnerable to a takeover. It was during that period, in 1993, that Randall Tobias became the CEO, joining the company from AT&T. Under his leadership, Eli Lilly shifted away from its historic focus on internal R&D, an approach that had left the company with a mediocre drug pipeline. To help the pharmaceutical giant escape its implementation trap, Tobias focused on four key BBB themes.

First, he created a highly active "borrow" strategy of contracts and alliances. For the fifteen years before he joined the company, Lilly had averaged fewer than two alliance deals a year. During Tobias's five years of leadership, that number increased to almost thirteen deals annually. These partnerships brought new products such as drugs for tuberculosis and Parkinson's disease into immediate sales, as well as a strong set of candidates for the longer-term pipeline. To support this newly launched "borrow" approach, Eli Lilly created an Office of Alliance Management, with staffers who helped evaluate potential partners and then actively managed those relationships once deals were formed.

Second, Tobias initiated a selective "buy" strategy. Two acquisitions in particular were noteworthy. The purchase of Sphinx Pharmaceuticals added combinatorial chemistry skills to the company's internal R&D capabilities for identifying candidate molecules, and the purchase of PCS Health Systems provided expansion into the growing pharmaceutical benefit-management business, with the goal of complementing the marketing of Lilly's drugs. These two deals offered expansion into fields where the company had little existing expertise.

Third, rather than cut back on the company's existing "build" strategy of internal development, Tobias actually increased Lilly's internal commitment. From 1993 to 1998, R&D expenditure almost doubled (from $950 million to more than $1.7 billion), reflecting an increase as a percentage of sales from 15 percent to 19 percent. At the same time, the company targeted its internal efforts more tightly, emphasizing higher-potential projects that built on existing strengths. This led to the launch and strong ongoing development support for the antidepressant blockbuster Zyprexa as well as diabetes drugs Humalog and Evista. Other projects led to major follow-on neurological and diabetes drugs such as Strattera, Cymbalta, and Forteo. These investments complemented the expansion opportunities available from Lilly's borrow and buy activities.

Fourth, while Lilly added new capabilities and products, the company also actively divested itself of products that no longer offered major growth opportunities. The medical-device business, which it had built through a series of acquisitions since the late 1970s, was spun off as Guidant in 1994, as were two smaller pharmaceutical units in 1995, and PCS Health Systems, which had not taken off as quickly as Lilly had hoped, was divested in 1998. Rather than sticking doggedly with PCS, which Lilly had acquired just a few years earlier, management decided to exit that business and reinvest the time and money in better opportunities.

These moves during the mid-1990s revitalized the company, with fivefold growth in market cap by the end of the decade, and helped build a foundation for longer-term success. Since then, "borrow" strategic alliances and contracts have continued at a rate of about thirteen deals per year; "buy" acquisitions, including three multibillion-dollar deals, have taken place about every two years; and "build" investments in internal R&D have continued to increase, reaching 24 percent of sales in 2015. Thanks to those activities, Eli Lilly has been able to maintain an active pipeline of new products to replace drugs such as Prozac, Zyprexa, and Cymbalta that have come off patent. Some new products have emerged from the company's internal Indianapolis Research Laboratories. Others, such as the erectile dysfunction drug Cialis, have been developed through alliances. Still others, such as the oncologic Erbitux, have been obtained via acquisition.

Today, Eli Lilly remains profitable and strongly independent, with revenues that have grown threefold from the early 1990s. Despite the tripling of revenue from 1993, however, Lilly had only 25 percent more employees in 2015. The leverage of the successful BBB strategy allowed the company to focus its internal efforts while searching globally for profitable external opportunities that complemented its internal strength.

It's important to stress that Eli Lilly's path to a multimodal growth strategy was not a short-term effort but a long, sustained initiative of ongoing change. Becoming proficient in deploying the BBB framework will take years. The alternative, though, is an existential threat, as implementation traps can easily lead to stagnant growth, declining market shares, depressed profits, and failure. H. G. Wells, the iconic author, said it clearly: "Adapt or perish, now as ever, is nature's inexorable imperative."

endnotes

1. L. Capron and W. Mitchell, *Build, Borrow, or Buy: Selecting Pathways for Growth* (Boston: Harvard Business Review Press, 2012).

2. S. Karim and W. Mitchell, "Innovation Through Acquisition and Internal Development: A Quarter-Century of Business Reconfiguration at Johnson & Johnson," *Long Range Planning* 37 (2004): 525–547.

3. L. Capron and W. Mitchell, "How to Grow Your Company: Why Best Practices and Implementation Excellence Won't Necessarily Save You," ChiefExecutive.net (May 21, 2013), available at http://chiefexecutive.net/how-to-grow-your-company.

4. L. Capron and W. Mitchell, "Find the Right Path," *Harvard Business Review* (July–August 2010): 102–107. See also L. Capron and W. Mitchell, *Build, Borrow, or Buy: Selecting Pathways for Growth* (Boston: Harvard Business Review Press, 2012).

5. These rules are adapted and extended from L. Capron and W. Mitchell, "How to Grow Your Company: Why Best Practices and Implementation Excellence Won't Necessarily Save You," ChiefExecutive.net (May 21, 2013), available at http://chiefexecutive.net/how-to-grow-your-company.

6. L. Capron and W. Mitchell, "Selection Capability: How Capability Gaps and Internal Social Frictions Affect Internal and External Strategic Renewal," *Organization Science* 20, no. 2 (2009): 294–312.

7. L. Mulotte, P. Dussauge, and W. Mitchell, "Does Collaboration Induce Spurious Learning and Overconfidence? Evidence from Independent vs. Collaborative Entry in the Global Aerospace Industry, 1944–2000," *Strategic Management Journal* 34, no. 3 (2013): 358–372.

8. See, for example, L. Capron, P. Dussauge, and W. Mitchell, "Resource Redeployment Following Horizontal Mergers and Acquisitions in Europe and North America, 1988–1992," *Strategic Management Journal* 19 (1998): 631–661; and S. Karim and W. Mitchell, "Innovation Through Acquisition and Internal Development: A Quarter-Century of Business Reconfiguration at Johnson & Johnson," *Long Range Planning* 37 (2004): 525–547.

9. L. Capron and W. Mitchell, "External Resource Sourcing: Does Experience Help Firms Select Governance Modes?" working paper (2014).

10. E. Vidal and W. Mitchell, "Adding by Subtracting: The Relationship Between Performance Feedback and Resource Reconfiguration Through Divestitures," *Organization Science* 26, no. 4 (2016): 1101–1118.

11. For a discussion of the nuances of reconfiguration, see S. Karim and L. Capron, "Adding, Redeploying, Recombining, and Divesting Resources and Business Units," *Strategic Management Society Journals* Virtual Issue on Reconfiguration (2015), available at http://onlinelibrary.wiley.com/journal/10.1002/%28ISSN%291097-0266/homepage/reconfiguration_vsi_introduction.htm.

missing the real competition

Michael Ryall

Evan Kristen Specialty Foods (EKSF) was an entrepreneurial venture that offered an innovative line of fresh herbs for
distribution through retail grocery chains. The novelty of
the product was in its ready-to-use nature: herbs such as
basil and thyme were offered fresh, washed, de-stemmed,
and sliced. To deliver on its consumer promise of year-
round availability with a two-week shelf life, EKSF had to
find innovative solutions to issues of technology (a proprietary processing facility to wash, de-stem, and slice delicate
herbs), distribution (an inventory-management system that
used FedEx to bypass the standard produce channel and
deliver overnight to the retail location, thereby increasing
shelf life by several days), and sourcing (identifying the
only microenvironment in the continental United States

capable of supplying a wide range of high-quality herbs year-round).

The early results were promising. At a time when grocery test-market sales of four to five cases per week per store were considered a success, test market sales averaged fifteen cases per week and, in some instances, more than twenty. Moreover, the margins on these products were far beyond anything being offered in the produce department. This meant that, for the first time, a produce entry could sustain a marketing program of sufficient substance to build a strong brand identity. In addition, the complex set of interlocking technologies and supplier relationships required to produce, process, and deliver the product to market meant that potential imitators would require considerable time to fit all these pieces together, and by then, EKSF would have the lead on building a national brand identity.

All of this pointed to the kind of investment opportunity that any venture capitalist would jump at, yet as the EKSF management team concluded its presentation to its venture backer E.M. Warburg Pincus, the reception was anything but enthusiastic. "I agree that these retail results are impressive," said the Warburg partner managing the case. "Even so, your business plan is fundamentally flawed. We may need to pull out as your venture capitalist."

What had happened?

fundamental strategy flaws

The EKSF situation highlights a feature present in many business settings, but especially in consumer products. Managers focus strongly on the customer end of the value chain, spending millions on market research to gauge the demand for new or updated products. Develop a product for which millions are willing to pay a hefty premium, with no imitators on the horizon, and success is guaranteed, right?

Wrong. The fundamental flaw in EKSF's strategy points toward a more general problem inherent in any partial analysis of a firm's competitive situation. By "partial," I mean an analysis that focuses on the competitive dynamics in one segment of the value chain (for example, consumer demand) at the expense of another (for example, input supply). Companies miss the real competition. Proper assessment of one's strategic position requires a refined understanding of *competitive intensity*—an understanding that must be grounded in a *complete* theory of value capture under competition.

The material in this chapter is motivated by a new and growing line of research in strategy that aims to refine our understanding of firm performance in competitive environments. The essential tool in this line is a mathematical framework known as the value capture model (VCM). Although this stream of work is relatively young by academic standards, it has already highlighted a number of important misperceptions and strategy blind spots with respect to how competition works.[1] In order to appreciate these and then to grasp the specific strategy flaw in the EKSF example, we must first step back and take in the picture of competition as conceived under the VCM framework.

a new perspective of competition

How much of the profit made by your firm is *guaranteed* by competition? It's an interesting question to ask, because most managers see competition as a persistent corrosive force on profitability. Competition may also have a positive, profit-boosting effect on performance, however. Which of these effects dominates for a given firm will depend on a balance in the productive powers of all the agents in its market. This is the overarching insight that arises from VCM's new perspective of competitive dynamics.[2]

Consider that firms create economic value by engaging in productive activities with other agents. When a firm is alone, its creative capacities are latent, unrealized. Only in the presence of other agents with creative capacities of their own can the potential to create economic value ever be actualized. In the simplest case, a firm has the potential to sell a product. This potential is worthless, however, without a buyer. Buyers are a particular class of agent—those with the potential to enjoy the use or consumption of products offered by other agents. Without sellers, these potentials are latent. Only together, when exercised through a sale, are the potentials of buyers and sellers actualized to produce real economic value.

An essential aspect of VCM is that it conceives of the firm and its transaction partners (customers, suppliers, and so on) as each possessing latent powers of value creation. A specific transaction identifies which agents actualize which of their potentials for what share of the resulting value created. Typically, an observed transaction is only one of myriad possibilities. Thus, the value captured by the agents in a transaction can be thought of as the inducement sufficient to voluntarily actualize the potentialities required of *that* transaction while leaving the others latent.

This perspective leads to several insights, some of which turn our assumptions about competition on their heads. First, competition arises from the mutual need of all parties engaged in a joint, economically productive activity to convince one another to actualize their latent powers in a certain way rather than some other way. This implies that there is *one* force of competition (not five, for example) that operates similarly throughout the market: on the firm as well as on its rivals, suppliers, and buyers. The iconic image of competition as a firm contending for buyers against its rivals omits the fact that in a symmetric sense, buyers may be similarly required to contend for transactions with the firm! This is all the more apparent in supplier, employee, and distributor relations.

Second, conceptualized in this way, we see that competition determines a *minimum* quantity of economic value that each agent *must* capture in order to ensure that it does not exercise its creative powers in other ways with different agents.[3] Here is the key: *The more substantial and extensive are a company's latent powers of value creation relative to the ones exercised in its actual transactions, the greater is this minimum—and the more competition works in its favor.* Because competition operates similarly for the firm's transaction partners (there is one force, remember), it increases the partners' minima as well. Holding the transaction constant, more competition of this kind reduces the value available for capture by the firm and hence imposes a *maximum* quantity of economic value the firm may capture in order to ensure that its transaction partners do not exercise their creative powers in different ways with other firms. Typically, all agents must part with some value to induce their partners not to actualize their creative powers in alternative transactions.

competitive intensity: determining the gap between floor and ceiling

The range of value-capture possibilities for a given agent is determined by this interplay between the latent and actualized productive capacities of everyone in the market. Competition for your transaction partners places a ceiling on the value you can capture. Competition for you creates a floor. The former corresponds to our traditional intuition. The latter is new. Taken together, they imply a novel conception of *competitive intensity*, namely the extent to which competition closes the gap between floor and ceiling. For a given agent, competition is at its most intense when the floor and the ceiling are equal— that is, when competition fully determines the quantity of value an agent must capture. At the other end of the spectrum, competition is least intense when it has no effect on an agent's value-capture possibilities.

The two ends of the spectrum are exemplified by two textbook cases: "perfect competition" and "pure bargaining." Perfect competition has come to mean situations in which free entry causes prices to be driven down to marginal cost, with the result of zero profit at the firm level. Under such conditions, the firm cannot demand more value, because competition for its buyers is so intense. If it does not relinquish all of the economic value created in its transactions with buyers, those buyers will simply exercise their creative powers with other firms. In other words, the firm's ceiling has been driven down to meet its floor at zero capture of economic value. Alternatively, in the textbook case of bilateral monopoly, only one buyer is interested in acquiring a product or service and only one seller exists to provide it. Here there are no alternatives for either party (other than abstaining from the transaction). In this situation, any split of the value created is consistent with competition (as there is no competition).

It is worth noting that the grim case of perfect competition, which is the one that normally comes to mind when we think about intense competition, is itself one-sided. There is another textbook case of intense competition that most firms would happily invite: monopolistic provision of a product under perfectly elastic demand. The key feature of perfectly elastic demand is that the firm's buyers are completely substitutable. Once again, as in the perfect-competition case, the firm's floor equals its ceiling, and competition fully determines the amount of value the firm captures. Now, the intensity is all on the side of the firm, with buyers vying for transactions with it, resulting in competition that guarantees that the firm can capture 100 percent of the value created. In other words, intense competition can work both ways.

Rarely, if ever, do real-world interactions fall at one extreme or the other. Generally, competition determines a *range* of value-capture possibilities for an agent. The narrower the range, the more intense is the competition surrounding an agent's actualized, economically productive interactions. The wider the range, the less intense is the competition for that agent and/or its transaction partners. When an agent's interval is nontrivial (that is, when its upper and lower bounds are not equal), we say the agent faces *competitive slack*. Again, most, if not all, agents face some competitive slack.

To summarize, competition for the firm guarantees it some minimum quantity of economic value (which may be equal to but is typically greater than zero), while competition for its transaction partners limits its capture to some maximum level (which may be equal to but is typically less than all the value created in the market). The exact amount of value a firm actually captures, then, is equal to the minimum guaranteed by competition plus some quantity of the slack between the minimum and the maximum. This formulation has implications for strategy.

competitive slack and the role of "persuasive resources"

We now know that the economic value captured by a firm—its economic profit—is equal to some amount guaranteed by competition plus some portion of its competitive slack. The total slack is determined by the firm's productive resources, the productive resources of the other agents in the market, and the interplay of the potentials of all these resources to create value through joint economic action. The portion of slack that the firm ultimately manages to capture is due to a category of resource that strategy scholars refer to as *persuasive*.

In its pure form, a persuasive resource is an item that does not create any economically productive potential for the firm. Rather, its sole function is to convince the firm's actual transaction partners to part with some of their own slack. Note the distinction: Competition is about a tension that arises between (1) the value created by actualizing the productive potentials among a set of transacting parties and (2) the need to identify a distribution of that value such that each of the parties has sufficient incentive to play the role necessary for its creation; persuasion is about bargaining over the share of remaining value once the implications of competition are fully resolved. For example, in the bilateral monopoly (one buyer and one seller), there are no appeals to competition; by definition, neither party has any alternative to the contemplated transaction. Here, an appeal to "fairness"—that is, to share the value equally—is an attempt at persuasion. An example of a persuasive resource would be an experienced salesperson with a special talent for convincing potential buyers to pay prices above their reservation values.

In the real world, resources typically embody both productive and persuasive capacities. For example, the services provided by salespeople—aligning products with customer needs, acting as go-betweens for clients and systems designers, expediting customer service, and so on—may create value with the firm's buyers and hence a resource that is productive. At the same time, the salesforce could be well trained in the art of persuasion. This productive/persuasive distinction is real and important. For example, even the most effective persuasive resources in the world would have no effect on value capture when competition is at its most intense (that is, when a firm's floor touches its ceiling and there is no slack at all). Other things being equal, the return on investment in persuasive resources is lower in settings of intense competition. In contrast, investing in productive resources that reduce the relative value of alternative options for the firm's transaction partners (for example, creating switching costs)—a move designed to increase the firm's competitive slack by reducing competition for the partners—is less attractive when the firm's persuasive resources are weak. Note that the efficacy of a firm's persuasive resources is always relative to the strength of the persuasive resources of that firm's transaction partners.

Finally, keep in mind that what counts as persuasion is everything that determines value capture outside of competition. Thus, while personal charm, appeals to fairness, and other forms of literal persuasion obviously fall into this category, organizational mechanisms and industry norms also count. For example, the sales technology may not allow pricing negotiation (for example, online retail), or deals might typically be determined through a sealed-bid auction (for example, construction projects). These institutions and norms have significant effects on the distribution of competitive slack. When we speak of persuasive resources, then, we mean to think in the broadest sense of how the competitive slack gets allocated (that is, even when we may not be able to point to special resources, per se).

mapping strategic positions

These two dimensions—competitive intensity and strength of resources (both productive and persuasive)— have significant implications for strategic positioning. As shown in Figure 10.1, the two dimensions map out four broad environments in which a firm may find itself operating. In the figure, the x-axis indicates the relative balance of a firm's resources. On the left, the firm is relying heavily on the resources that create potentials to generate value. This implies a strategic focus on fostering competition for the firm, pushing that ceiling as high as it will go. Firms on the right side of the x-axis have well-developed persuasive resources. They are positioned to capture any value that remains unaccounted for by competition—that is, the value in their competitive slack. The y-axis indicates the degree of competitive intensity surrounding the firm as it participates in its complex systems of relations to produce economic value. Moving from top to bottom, competitive intensity is increasing, and with that movement comes a corresponding drop in the efficacy of persuasive resources. Breaking the space into four broad categories of competitive position results in the following quadrants.

QI: Outgunned at the Table. In the upper left quadrant, a firm encounters substantial competitive slack. The problem, however, is that its persuasive resources are weak. In essence, the firm's persuasive resources are out of alignment with the competitive intensity it faces, and the firm ends up "leaving money on the table." A natural reaction to being in this location is to pump up one's productive resources, to increase the potential to create value outside of the firm's present set of transaction partners in order to foster

Figure 10.1: Strategic Positioning

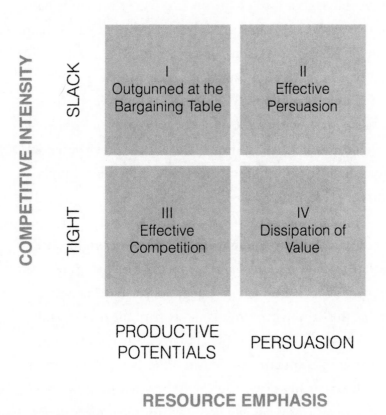

competition *for* the firm and thereby to push its minimum upwards. Notice that to the extent such a strategy is successful, the firm moves to QIII. Examples of such moves include vertical product differentiation (by increasing the appeal of the product throughout the market, beyond the set of active buyers, competition for the firm increases) and capacity consolidation (eliminating some capacity increases the competitive intensity for that which remains). Alternatively, the firm can shift its emphasis to develop strong persuasive resources—an attempt to move to QII. When General Motors invests in salesperson training for its dealers, for example, the automaker is increasing its persuasive resources in hopes of swaying actual car buyers at the point of sale to part with value above and beyond the prices at which the dealers could surely sell to some other potential buyer (i.e., the minimum prices determined by competition for GM automobiles).

QII: Effective Persuasion. In the upper right quadrant, persuasive resources and competitive intensity are well aligned. Here, value capture is high, as persuasive resources enable the firm to capture a large share of the overall value, most of which is open to persuasive efforts because of the low level of competitive intensity. The canonical example is a situation in which each member in the network of transacting firms is equally necessary for the project to proceed (as might be the case in the production of an innovative technology platform). This is the quadrant in which simply finding ways to "add value"—without worrying at all about simultaneously increasing the potential to create value with others so as to foster competitive intensity—works.

QIII: Effective Competition. In the lower left quadrant, firms foster high competitive intensity with little focus on persuasive resources. This is an efficient quadrant in which to operate because the development of persuasive capabilities matches (and fosters) the competitive situation. When competition is tight, persuasion is of little value. In this quadrant, competition works to ensure a large share of the economic value (for example, the monopolist facing perfectly elastic demand), which is a very desirable position, indeed. Here, the typical dynamic is a virtuous cycle in the sense that competition prevents the development of any gap between the firm's maximum and minimum, which prevents movement toward QI, thus ensuring that a firm has no reason to strengthen its persuasive resources.

QIV: Value Dissipation. In the lower right quadrant, a firm's persuasive resources are, again, out of sync with its competitive situation. Here, the firm has strong persuasive resources but little competitive slack upon which to applythose resources. As long as the firm remains in this position, whatever costs it incurs to develop or maintain its resources are wasted. One option for the firm to move to QII is to create more economic value with its present partners, which has the effect of raising its maximum above its minimum. The resulting slack is then available for capture via the firm's superior persuasive resources. Another possibility in moving to QII is to neutralize the latent potentials of its transaction partners—that is, to reduce or eliminate its partners' alternative opportunities to create value in exclusion of the firm. One such approach is the creation of switching costs. For example, when pharmaceutical companies create specialized equipment required for the delivery of their products to hospital patients, the potential of current hospital clients to create value with alternative pharmaceutical suppliers is reduced (because the switching costs must be factored in). Finally, a firm in QIV moves to QIII by shifting its resource emphasis to the productive side and away from persuasive resources. For example, between 2009 and 2013, pharmaceuticals witnessed massive industry-wide reductions in sales teams. One of the significant factors contributing to this was increased competitive intensity resulting from a major shift from individual physician-prescribers to large health plans. That shift forced pharmaceuticals to compete for big-buyer business, which moved them from QII to QIV. As the pharmas reacted by eliminating their persuasive resources, they were moved from QIV to QIII.

In considering these positions, it's important to note that moves from one side of the *x*-axis to the other are typically quite difficult. After all, a firm's present balance of resources is the consequence of a complex, history-dependent evolution of factors involving relationships between the firm's technology, its knowledge resources, its culture, its reputation, the structure and norms associated with its partner transactions, and so on. Although every situation is unique and should be attended to with careful discernment, movement from QI to

QIII and from QIV to QII are going to be the most strategically efficacious.

the problem for EKSF

Returning to the example in the introduction of this
chapter, what the company's managers failed to grasp (and
the Warburg partner apparently did) was that EKSF's
strategic positioning was fundamentally flawed. Situated
high in QI, EKSF faced a serious misalignment: massive
slack on the one hand, and a total emphasis on competitive
resources on the other. To appreciate this, note that, although the close-fitting pieces of the EKSF business model
may have kept imitators at bay, they also had a crucial effect on the strategic positioning of the company. The EKSF
promise of year-round availability could be met by supply
from only a *single* farm—the only farm that happened to
grow herbs in the aforementioned microenvironment. In
order for EKSF to create full value with its retail customers,
it *had* to actualize its own productive capacity in conjunc-
tion with *that* particular farm. In effect, the incredible
competitive intensity for EKSF products on the retail side
was really competitive intensity for the EKSF-farm pair.
Although competition would ensure that enormous value
would be captured from consumers (in the form of high
prices for EKSF products), it provided no determination
of how that value would be split between EKSF and the
farm. The two parties needed each other in this endeavor,

and perhaps EKSF was more dependent on the farm than the other way around, because the farm already had an on-going business to which it could always revert. That is, the farm had a potential to create value without EKSF.

Consider the following scenario. Everything runs smoothly during the early stages of a nationwide EKSF rollout. Then, as the level of market success becomes clear, it dawns on the farmers just how critical they are. At this point, threats and demands for higher raw-material prices suddenly appear. Warburg was right to be worried. Dependence on the farm implied a potentially unsustainable position for EKSF—one that had the potential of destroying the return on Warburg's investment. One possibility would have been a contract designed to lock in raw-material prices (that is, an attempt to move from QI to QII); however, should EKSF become as successful as anticipated, the incentive for the farm to renege on such a contract might prove irresistible. Another solution would have been to backward-integrate by purchasing the farm, but this would have required even greater funding from Warburg. Or EKSF could have, in parallel with its national rollout, convinced other nearby farms to divert some production capacity to herbs. This would then have created new potentials for EKSF to create value, thereby increasing the competitive intensity surrounding its operations in a positive way. Each of these last two strategies would have involved a strategic move from QI to QIII.

Had the EKSF management known of the fundamental flaw in its strategy, it could have acted proactively to solve these issues in advance. Unfortunately, though, the initial focus was on proof of concept for the production and retail dimensions of the business model. As the model came together and as the size of the potential value pie became apparent (the latter implying a huge incentive for the farm to hold up EKSF), the experienced Warburg partner clearly grasped the danger. Ultimately, funding was pulled, and as a result, EKSF ceased to exist.

Although the story of EKSF is an extreme (and somewhat oversimplified) example, many firms have fundamental flaws in their competitive strategies. Like EKSF, they might be residing high in QI, unaware that their suppliers could soon be abandoning them. Or they might be located in QIV, wastefully investing precious resources in persuasive capabilities that provide no return. The VCM framework presented in this chapter can help managers identify and avoid missing the real competition. That said, VCM is a relatively new approach, and the field of strategy is a complex domain. I expect that future refinements of the framework will enable leaders to better chart the strategic directions of their organizations.

endnotes

1. 1. Interested readers are directed toward the pioneering contributions of A.M. Brandenburger and H.W. Stuart, "Value-Based Business

Strategy," *Journal of Economics & Management Strategy* 5, no. 1 (1996): 5–24; and A. Brandenburger and B. Nalebuff, *Co-Opetition* (New York: Doubleday, 1996). The former is directed to an academic audience and the latter to business practitioners. For a recent review, see J.S. Gans and M. Ryall, "The Value Capture Model: A Strategic Management Review," *Strategic Management Review*, 2017 (forthcoming).

2. For an introduction, see M.D. Ryall, "The New Dynamics of Competition," *Harvard Business Review* (June 2013).

3. Note that "economic value captured" means the same thing as "economic profit." The "value captured" formulation is useful in highlighting the connection between the creation of economic value and its distribution among the agents involved in that creation.

11

conclusion: survive and thrive

Joshua Gans and Sarah Kaplan

This book has dealt with the fears that senior managers face in their businesses. Those fears are not unreasonable, and because these threats behind these fears come from a diverse set of causes, they can feel overwhelming. Not surprisingly, leaders have plenty to keep them up at night.

The authors of these chapters are all business-school professors. Our students are leaders of tomorrow. In effect, our job is to prepare our students for those future sleepless nights, but our hope is that they mainly get good nights' rest.

At the same time, we do not want to minimize genuine fear with platitudes. Instead, our approach is to focus on structured anticipation. In these chapters, we use research to understand threats, investigate solutions, and evaluate what really can get the job done. Each chapter of this book has focused on a particular threat. Each chapter has also have pointed you toward research-based approaches to the challenges that underlie those fears. The chapters draw out four mistakes that companies commonly make and, collectively, propose two actions and two cautions for leaders trying to anticipate and react to threats.

Our goal: provide step-by-step actions to help companies stay alive. In this book, executives will have found principles and practices for anticipating potential threats and creating responses that permit their businesses to not only survive but thrive.

Our job is not yet done, however. This book is a snapshot of the state of knowledge as it exists in 2017. Around the world, business schools employ research professors like us for a reason: The world is changing. Old fears disappear, and new ones arise. Some solutions are familiar; some require innovation. All require a rigorous and dispassionate approach to their evaluation—but simply put, you cannot find a strategy for a sustainable business without sustainable knowledge. The system that we are a part of is dedicated to that.

This book is a living document. Our intentions and hopes are to update it as new research comes to light. Please come back from time to time and see how it is going at www.SurviveandThriveBook.ca. Sustainable knowledge is not static, and so continuous learning means dipping back into the research from time to time.

author biographies

Ajay Agrawal is the Peter Munk Professor of Entrepreneurship at Rotman, where he conducts research on the economics of artificial intelligence, science policy, entrepreneurial finance, and geography of innovation. Professor Agrawal is a research associate at the National Bureau of Economic Research in Cambridge, Massachusetts; cofounder of the Next 36 and NextAI; and founder of the Creative Destruction Lab.

Anne Bowers is associate professor at Rotman. She researches how classification and rating systems shape market outcomes. She also studies how competition among third-party intermediaries affects their ratings and reports, with a particular interest in financial markets.

Kevin Bryan is assistant professor at Rotman. His work consists primarily of applied theoretical analyses of innovation, generally supported by detailed qualitative historical investigation. At present, he is particularly interested in questions related to which research lines inventors and firms pursue, and how "directional inefficiency" in these choices can be mitigated. He maintains a side interest in studying the history of thought, the history of the Industrial Revolution, and social scientific methodology.

Alberto Galasso is associate professor of strategic management in the Department of Management at the University of Toronto Mississauga, with a cross-appointment to Rotman. His research is focused on the determinants of innovative activity, the management of innovation, and the functioning of markets for technology.

Joshua Gans holds the Jeffrey S. Skoll Chair in Technical Innovation and Entrepreneurship and is a professor, as well as area coordinator of strategic management at Rotman (with a cross-appointment in the Department of Economics). His research is focused primarily on understanding the economic drivers of innovation and scientific progress, with core interests in digital strategy and antitrust policy. Joshua is Chief Economist in Rotman's Creative Destruction Lab, is managing director of the Core Research consultancy, and writes regularly for Forbes, HBR, and Digitopoly.

Sarah Kaplan is the University of Toronto Distinguished Professor of Gender & the Economy, as well as Director, Institute for Gender + the Economy at Rotman. She is a coauthor of the bestselling business book *Creative Destruction*. Her research explores how organizations participate in and respond to the emergence of new fields and technologies. Her studies examine biotechnology, communications, financial services, nanotechnology, and, most recently, the field emerging at the nexus of gender and finance. Her focus on gender equality is in understanding it as an innovation challenge.

Anita M. McGahan holds the Rotman Chair in Management at Rotman. She is cross appointed to the Munk School of Global Affairs and the medical school's Department of Physiology; serves as President of the Academy of Management; participates as faculty in the MacArthur Research Network on Opening Governance; and is Chief Economist at the Massachusetts General Hospital Division for Global Health and Human Rights. Her credits include four books and over 150 articles, case studies, notes and other published material on competitive advantage, industry evolution, and financial performance. McGahan's current research emphasizes entrepreneurship in the public interest and innovative collaboration between public and private organizations. She is also pursuing a long-standing interest in the inception of new industries, particularly in global health.

Will Mitchell holds the Anthony S. Fell Chair in New Technologies and Commercialization at Rotman. He studies business dynamics in developed and emerging markets, investigating how businesses change as their competitive environments change and, in turn, how business changes contribute to ongoing corporate and social performance. Will teaches courses in corporate strategy, emerging market strategy, entrepreneurial strategy, and pharmaceutical and health-sector strategy. He serves as a board member of Neuland Laboratories, Ltd. (Hyderabad).

A. Rebecca Reuber is professor of strategic management at Rotman. Her research focuses on the growth strategies of entrepreneurial organizations, particularly those based on digital technologies. Her research has focused on reputation development in young firms, and the internationalization of new ventures.

Michael Ryall is professor at Rotman. His primary research interest is in the theoretical foundations of business strategy. This work develops mathematical models designed to analyze the causes of persistent performance differences between firms under competition. His other research interests include the sources and evolution of group learning, joint commitment, and shared beliefs in organizations and their effects on performance.

András Tilcsik is associate professor of strategic management at Rotman, as well as a faculty fellow at the Michael Lee-Chin Family Institute for Corporate Citizenship. He studies the organizational aspects of work, employment, and occupations. He is coauthor of the forthcoming book *Meltdown*.

index

Note: Page numbers in italics refer to figures.

CPSIA information can be obtained
at www.ICGtesting.com
Printed in the USA
LVOW07s1030061017
551362LV00005B/10/P